S0-ACL-855

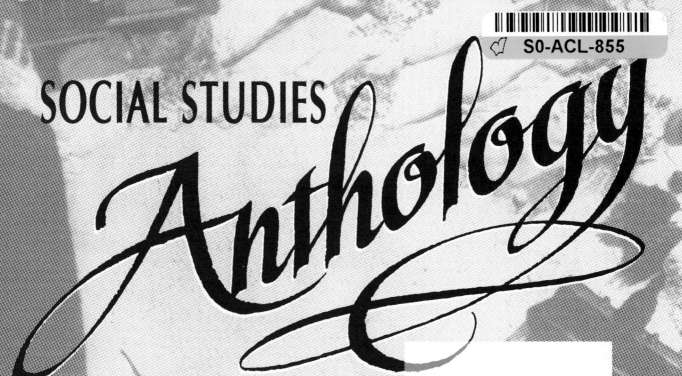

# SOCIAL STUDIES
# *Anthology*

## THE WORLD AROUND US

The children on the cover photograph are reciting our country's Pledge of Allegiance. The United States has a great variety of communities and cultures which are shown by many things, including antique toys, a cornhusk doll, and a Navajo blanket.

## MACMILLAN/McGRAW-HILL SCHOOL PUBLISHING COMPANY
### NEW YORK    CHICAGO    COLUMBUS

## PROGRAM AUTHORS •

**Dr. James A. Banks**
Professor of Education and Director of the Center for
  Multicultural Education
University of Washington
Seattle, Washington

**Dr. Barry K. Beyer**
Professor of Education and American Studies
George Mason University
Fairfax, Virginia

**Dr. Gloria Contreras**
Professor of Education and Director of the Office of
  Multicultural Affairs
University of North Texas
Denton, Texas

**Jean Craven**
District Coordinator of Curriculum Development
Albuquerque Public Schools
Albuquerque, New Mexico

**Dr. Gloria Ladson-Billings**
Assistant Professor of Education
University of Wisconsin
Madison, Wisconsin

**Dr. Mary A. McFarland**
Director of Staff Development and Instructional
  Coordinator of Social Studies, K-12
Parkway School District
Chesterfield, Missouri

**Dr. Walter C. Parker**
Associate Professor of Social Studies Education and
  Director of the Center for the Study of Civic
  Intelligence
University of Washington
Seattle, Washington

## CONTENT CONSULTANTS •

**Yvonne Beamer**
Resource Specialist
Native American Education Program
New York, New York

**Mario T. Garcia**
Professor of History and American Studies
Yale University
New Haven, Connecticut

**Valerie Ooka Pang**
Associate Professor, School of Teacher Education
San Diego State University
San Diego, California

**Clifford E. Trafzer**
Professor of Ethnic Studies and Director of Native
  American Studies
University of California
Riverside, California

## GRADE-LEVEL CONSULTANTS •

**Jo-Ann Potter**
Elementary Teacher
North Hero Elementary School
North Hero, Vermont

**Jonathan Powell**
Elementary Teacher
Emerson Open Magnet School
Wichita, Kansas

**Connie Hill**
Elementary Teacher
Wheatland Elementary School
Naperville, Illinois

**Helen Holley**
Elementary Teacher
Epic Elementary School
Birmingham, Alabama

## ACKNOWLEDGMENTS •

*The publisher gratefully acknowledges permission to reprint the following copyrighted material:*

"Why We Have Dogs in Hopi Villages" from AND IT IS STILL THAT WAY Legends told by Arizona Indian Children with notes by Byrd Baylor. Copyright © 1976 by Byrd Baylor. Published by Trails West Press, Santa Fe, New Mexico. Reprinted by permission of the author.

Excerpts from WHAT ARE YOU FIGURING NOW? A STORY ABOUT BENJAMIN BANNEKER by Jeri Ferris. Text copyright © 1988 by Jeri Ferris. Published by Carolrhoda Books, Inc., Minneapolis, MN. Used with permission. All rights reserved.

*(continued on page 137)*

Macmillan/McGraw-Hill School Division
10 Union Square East
New York, New York 10003

Printed in the United States of America
ISBN 0-02-146125-2
1 2 3 4 5 6 7 8 9  POH  99 98 97 96 95 94 93 92

# TABLE OF *Contents*

USING YOUR ANTHOLOGY      vi

**UNIT 1 LEARNING ABOUT COMMUNITIES**      1

*The Fourth*
poem by Shel Silverstein      2

*Kwanzaa*
selection from a nonfiction story by
Deborah M. Newton Chocolate      3

*My Best Friend, Mee-Yung Kim*
selection from a story by Dianne MacMillan
and Dorothy Freeman      7

*Music, Music for Everyone*
story and art by Vera B. Williams      12

*Mr. Griggs' Work*
story by Cynthia Rylant      18

*John Henry*
tall tale retold by Ezra Jack Keats      21

*Where the River Begins*
story by Thomas Locker      25

*Ming Lo Moves the Mountain*
story by Arnold Lobel      28

**UNIT 2 OUR FIRST COMMUNITIES**      33

*The Great Race*
Sioux and Cheyenne story retold by Paul Goble      34

*Before You Came This Way*
poem by Byrd Baylor      38

*Why We Have Dogs in Hopi Villages*
legend retold by Hopi children with Byrd Baylor      42

*Cross and Sword*
selection from a play by Paul Green      45

*. . . If You Sailed on the Mayflower*
selection from a nonfiction book by Ann
McGovern      47

*In Good Old Colony Times*
traditional Colonial song      50

☐ = audio cassette

**UNIT 3**

**TYPES OF COMMUNITIES**                                    **51**

*The Best Town in the World*
story by Byrd Baylor                                         52

*Yagua Days*
selection from a story by Cruz Martel                       58

*Rudolph Is Tired of the City*
poem by Gwendolyn Brooks                                    63

*Rhyme-Time Fun*
traditional rhymes                                          64

*Picking Berries*
poem by Aileen Fisher                                       67

*How Pizza Came to Queens*
story by Dayal Kaur Khalsa                                  68

*The Patchwork Quilt*
selection from a story by Valerie Flournoy                  71

*Sing a Song of People*
poem by Lois Lenski                                         77

*In a Neighborhood in Los Angeles*
poem by Francisco X. Alarcón                                78

*The City Blues*
traditional blues song                                      80

*Working on an Assembly Line*
interview with Chuck Hilt from a
nonfiction book by Neil Johnson                             81

*The House on Hillside La*
selection from a story by Johanna Hurwitz                   83

*Field*
poem by Frank Asch                                          86

**UNIT 4**

**COMMUNITIES HAVE HISTORIES**                              **87**

*. . . If You Lived at the Time of the Great
San Francisco Earthquake*
selection from a nonfiction book by Ellen
Levine                                                      88

*San Francisco*
two poems by Langston Hughes                                92

📼 *Bringing the Rain to Kapiti Plain*
Nandi tale retold by Verna Aardema    93

📼 *Down in a Coal Mine*
traditional miners' song    97

*In Coal Country*
selection from a story by Judith Hendershot    98

*Childtimes*
selection from an autobiography by Eloise
Greenfield and Lessie Jones Little    103

📼 *Familytimes*
two poems by Eloise Greenfield and
Lessie Jones Little    107

*50 Simple Things Kids Can Do to Save
the Earth*
selection from a nonfiction book by John
Javna and The EarthWorks Group    108

**UNIT**
**⑤ COMMUNITIES HAVE GOVERNMENTS 111**

*Julio in the Lion's Den*
selection from a story by Johanna Hurwitz    112

*. . . If You Were There When They Signed
the Constitution*
selection from a nonfiction book by
Elizabeth Levy    117

*The Rights of the Child*
a Declaration by the United Nations    122

*What Are You Figuring Now?*
selection from a biography of Benjamin
Banneker by Jeri Ferris    124

📼 *Rise and Shine (Give Yourself a Chance)*
song by Professor Rap    129

**Index by Category**    132
**Index by Title**    133
**Index by Author**    134
**Index by Subject**    135
**Acknowledgments**    137

# USING YOUR *Anthology*

In *Communities Near and Far* you will be reading about many different people, places, and times. This Anthology, or collection of writings by different people, will make the information in your textbook come to life in a special way. The Anthology includes stories, tall tales, songs, biographies, poems, and games. As you read these selections, you will be able to see, feel, and hear what it is like to live in other communities. Your Anthology will even take you back into the past and help you feel what it was like to live in other times! The selections in your Anthology will help you to better understand communities in the past and present, both near and far.

**INTRODUCTION •**
Gives you background information about the selection and tells you what kind of writing it is. Is it fiction or nonfiction? Is it a poem or a song? The introduction also asks you a question to think about as you read the selection.

**DEFINITIONS •**
Gives you the meanings of difficult words

**CONCLUSION •**
Tells you what happened next and asks you to think further about the selection

**CASSETTE LOGO •**
Tells you that the selection appears on the Anthology Cassette

**TEXTBOOK LINK •**
Tells you which chapter and lesson in your textbook the document is linked to

**SOURCE •**
Tells you where the selection came from

Use with Chapter 7, Lesson 1

## Picking Berries
### by Aileen Fisher

Long ago, people lived off the land, picking wild plants and hunting wild animals. Berries were one of their main foods. Today, many kinds of berries are grown on fruit farms and others still grow wild in rural areas. In the poem below, Aileen Fisher describes a day spent picking berries. How does the poem make you feel you were there?

All day long
we picked and picked.

The sun was strong,
the bushes pricked.

The berries grew
in **brambly** places
where twigs untied
my sneaker laces.

brambly: full of thorns

We picked and picked
and picked some more.
The sun blazed down,
my arms got sore,

And then all night
as time went ticking
I dreamed I still
kept picking, picking.

Picking berries by hand can be lots of fun. But picking berries day after day, as many farm workers do, is very hard work. Have you ever picked berries? What's your favorite kind?

Source: Lee Bennett Hopkins, ed., *On the Farm.* Boston: Little, Brown, 1991.

67

# LEARNING ABOUT COMMUNITIES

*After that we played and played. We made mistakes, but we played like a real band. The little lanterns came on. Everyone danced.*

from *Music, Music for Everyone*
by Vera B. Williams

 # THE FOURTH

## by Shel Silverstein

*The Fourth of July is the birthday of our country—the United States of America. Americans celebrate this birthday in many different ways. But there's one thing almost everybody does on the Fourth of July—they watch fireworks. This poem is about how fireworks look and sound. Can you see how the poet does this? First read the poem from start to finish. Then read it again reading only the words printed in small letters. Then read it a third time reading only the words in capitals. How does the poem sound different?*

Oh
CRASH!

my
BASH!

it's
BANG!

the
ZANG!
Fourth

WHOOSH!

of

BAROOOM!

July
WHEW!

*The Fourth of July is more than just fireworks. It's a day to remember and celebrate our country's independence. It's also a day to think about freedom and equality for all people around the world.*

Source: Lillian Morrison, *Rhythm Road: Poems to Move To.* New York: Crowell, 1988.

# Kwanzaa

**by Deborah M. Newton Chocolate**

*People of all cultures and backgrounds celebrate special holidays. Many African Americans celebrate the holiday Kwanzaa, or the African harvest festival. By celebrating this holiday they are sharing the customs and beliefs of their African ancestors. In the selection below, a young boy tells about how his family celebrates Kwanzaa. What African traditions are part of the holiday?*

Every year, from the day after Christmas until the first day of the new year, our family celebrates Kwanzaa!

*Kwanzaa* is an African-American celebration. The name comes from the East African Swahili word *kwanzaa*, meaning "the first." Kwanzaa is a gathering time, just like Thanksgiving or a family **reunion**.

Many of our ancestors were farmers. The seven **principles** of Kwanzaa celebrate African harvesttime and a way of life handed down to us by our ancestors and parents.

In keeping with the spirit of Kwanzaa, Mama wears a *lappa* or *buba*, which is an African dress. She braids her hair into beautiful **cornrows**.

Daddy and Allen and I wear *dashikis* or *kanzus*. This is **traditional** dress for African men. We wear *kofis* on our heads and beads around our necks.

**reunion:** gathering of friends or relatives after a long absence

**principles:** beliefs

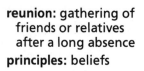

**cornrows:** rows of small, tight braids

**traditional:** according to custom

We decorate our home in the black, red, and green colors of Kwanzaa. We fly our *bendera*, or flag. Black is for the color of our people. Red is for our continuing struggle. And green is for the lush, rolling hills of our beautiful motherland, Africa. Green also is the color of hope, represented by African-American children. Together we prepare a table for the Kwanzaa *karamu*, or feast.

Mama puts a *mkeke*, or straw mat, on the table. Aunt Ife wove it for the celebration. In Africa it is an old custom to make things by hand. The handwoven mkeke stands for our past.

On top of the mkeke, Daddy puts a *kinara* or candle holder. The kinara is the holder of the flame. It stands for all black people, both past and present. The *mishumaa saba*, or seven candles in the kinara, stand for the seven Kwanzaa principles that teach us how to live. . . .

We show our love for our family through the *zawadi*, or gifts, we make. On the night before the last day of Kwanzaa, we give our parents gifts that remind us of Africa and our African-American ancestors. Allen and I earn our gifts by keeping the promises we made in the past year.

Each day, from sunrise to sunset, we do not eat. In the evening we gather in a circle around the karamu table. We share our home and food with family and friends, just as our ancestors shared the fruits of the hunt and the harvest.

Each night a candle is lit and one of the seven Kwanzaa principles is recited. On the first day of Kwanzaa, Daddy lights the black candle in the center of the kinara.

"Harambee!" he says.

"Harambee!" we answer. He recites the first principle of the *nguzo saba*, the seven principles of Kwanzaa. "*Umoja* means **unity**," says Daddy. "On this first day of

unity: togetherness

4

Kwanzaa, let us remember the importance of unity in the family. Let us love one another and stand up for one another. Let us honor our ancestors by celebrating our past."

We pass the *kikombe cha umoja*, or unity cup. We pour a libation, an offering to the memory of our ancestors, in the direction of the four winds—north, south, east, and west. And then, to honor our ancestors and in the spirit of unity, each person takes a sip. . . .

On the second day of Kwanzaa, Uncle Buddy lights a red candle in the kinara. "Always do the right thing," says Uncle Buddy. "Always stand up for what is right. This is what *kujichagulia*, or self-determination, means."

Uncle Buddy passes the *kikombe*, or cup. He recalls the days when he was a boy living on a sharecropping farm down south. He tells us stories about our grandfathers. He remembers the name of the village in Africa where his great-great grandmother was born.

"*Habari gani?*" ("What's the news?") greets Mama.

"*Ujima!*" everyone answers.

"Today I light the third candle of Kwanzaa for ujima!"

The glow from the flame dances across Mama's dark face. Shadows fill the room. Mama takes an ear of corn from the basket. "Ujima stands for **collective work** and **responsibility**. Our corn," she explains, "reminds us of the harvest that comes from ujima. Without work, there is no reward, no harvest for our people."

**collective work:** work done by a group
**responsibility:** job or duty

A family photo album, a cane-bottomed basket, a **flatiron**, and a set of wedding rings are some of the things that have been handed down in our family from generation to generation. We hear the story that goes with each of them. There is a top hat that belonged to my great-great grandfather, and a feathered headband that belonged to my great-great grandmother. Our great-great grandparents once sang and danced in traveling stage shows across the South.

**flatiron:** an object made of iron, often heated and used to brand something

Mufaro stands behind the kinara and lights the candle for the fourth celebration day, a red one, for *ujamma*. "Ujamma means '**cooperative economics.**' My family honors ujamma by helping me finish school. When I become a doctor, I'll come back to the community and help out."

**cooperative economics:** a way of producing goods and services where people work together and help each other

*Nia* means "purpose." On the fifth day, I light a green candle. I greet everyone with, "Harambee!"

"Harambee!" they answer.

"I have a purpose, no matter how small. My purpose is to keep promises and to honor my ancestors and parents." Both Mama and Daddy give me a great big hug after the kikombe cha umoja is passed around.

On New Year's Eve we celebrate the sixth principle of Kwanzaa, which is *kuumba*, or creativity. We work on the gifts we will exchange. There is more music and song and dance. Some of the music is African and some of it is African-American. Cousin Ebon plays a thumb piano. Uncle Will dances a **cakewalk** to it.

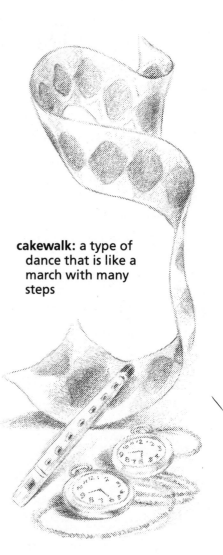

**cakewalk:** a type of dance that is like a march with many steps

Later that evening, we present our gifts. Allen and I give Mama a tie-dyed red, black, and green *gele*, or head wrap, made in art class. For Daddy we have a hand-carved flute.

Mama and Daddy surprise us with pocket watches that once belonged to our grandfathers.

After midnight, in the early morning of New Year's Day, Grandma Lela lights the last candle in honor of Kwanzaa. She recites the principle of *imani*, which means "faith."

"It is up to us to keep the faith of our ancestors. We must always stand together and be strong."

*The seven principles of Kwanzaa can have meaning for everyone. Think about one of the principles you read about. What does it mean? Why is it important?*

Source: Deborah M. Newton Chocolate, *Kwanzaa*. Chicago: Childrens Press, 1990.

# My Best Friend, Mee-Yung Kim

**by Dianne MacMillan and Dorothy Freeman**

*In large cities such as Los Angeles, California, there are people who have moved to the United States from many different countries. Some of these people from other countries settle in neighborhoods with others who share the same customs and holidays. In this selection from a story, a girl named Bonnie learns about the customs of a Korean-American classmate, Mee-Yung Kim. Mee-Yung Kim takes Bonnie with her to the Korean Harvest Festival parade in a Los Angeles neighborhood called Koreatown. As you read, imagine Mee-Yung Kim is in your class. What would you ask her about Korean customs and holidays?*

Mee-Yung Kim and I sat next to each other in social studies. I didn't know her very well until the "Salad Bowl" project. That was when we became best friends.

"There are people from many countries in this class," Mr. Clark, our teacher said. "That's one of the good things about living in Los Angeles. We're a mixture like a salad in a bowl!" Then he gave us an assignment. "If your parents were born in this country, choose a partner whose parents came from another country. Try to find out about customs that are different from those of other Americans. Are the same holidays celebrated?

How are things done at home? Later you'll report to the class on what you learn from each other."

I turned to ask Mee-Yung Kim to be my partner because she's Korean American. "Want to work together?" I asked.

"Sure, Bonnie. I was just going to ask you," she said. We decided to report on Mee-Yung's family.

Mee-Yung is really an American. She was born in the United States, but her parents were born in Korea. She says that her family has some Korean ways and some American ways.

Her father's a doctor. Most of his patients are Korean, so he speaks Korean to them. Her mother works in a bank and speaks English there.

At afternoon recess Mee-Yung said, "There's a Korean Harvest Festival parade next Saturday. You could see a lot of Korean customs there."

"I'd love to go to it!" I said.

"Great! You'll like the floats! My sister Alina and I are riding on one," she said.

I got up early on Saturday. I was excited about the festival. I took my camera to take pictures for our report.

At Mee-Yung's house, she and her sister came out to meet me. They were wearing long, beautiful dresses. Mee-Yung's was white on top and had a pink skirt with gold trimming.

She whirled to show the dress. Then she smiled at her sister and said to me, "This is Alina. She's in seventh grade." Alina's dress was all white with blue and gold borders on the sleeves and skirt. I was glad I had my camera to take their picture.

Alina said, "Korean clothes are called hanbok."

A tall, pretty woman came out of the house and Mee-Yung introduced her mother, Mrs. Chung. I wondered why she wasn't called Mrs. Kim, but I didn't ask.

Mee-Yung said, "The parade's going to be in Koreatown. That's the Korean business section of Los Angeles. My father's office is there."

When we got to Koreatown, I couldn't read the signs. Mee-Yung said they were in Chinese and Korean. At the place where the parade was starting, there were hundreds of girls and boys in bright colored hanbok, Korean clothing. I recognized Chi-Won Lee, a boy from our class. He was wearing a white shirt, baggy white pants, and a green belt. "Hi!" he said to Mee-Yung. "Which float are you riding on?"

"The Korean **Chamber of Commerce** float," Alina said. Then she looked at me and added, "That's an honor because they're in charge of the festival."

chamber of commerce: a group of local business leaders

"That's my Tae Kwon Do class." Chi-Won pointed to a group of boys that were lining up to be in the parade. "Wait until you see what we're going to do! Watch for me in the parade."

We went to the place where the floats were waiting. Mee-Yung and Alina climbed on the Korean Chamber of Commerce float. Mrs. Chung helped them spread their skirts. They practiced waving to the crowd.

I sat on the curb and looked around at all the Korean stores. Behind me was a furniture store. In the store window were shiny black tables and chests.

The floats were decorated with plastic flower petals. Mee-Yung's float had one huge flower with heart-shaped petals. Mee-Yung and Alina and other Korean girls sat by the petals.

After a while Mee-Yung's mother sat on the curb with me. When the floats started to move, we stood up to get a better view. Most of the people on the floats were children. Some were very little, but they smiled and waved.

On the front of the Korean Air Lines' float, a large orange-and-black tiger looked like he was waving his paw. "He's Hodori, the Korean **mascot** for the 1988 **Seoul** Olympics," Mrs. Chung said.

mascot: pet animal
**Seoul**: capital of South Korea

Another float had a white grand piano on it. All the children riding on this float were dressed in white and the flower petals were white and silver.

"That's Mee-Yung's music teacher playing the piano," Mrs. Chung said.

"I've never seen a piano in a parade before," I said.

"Almost all Korean children take music lessons. Music is really important to us," she said. . . .

I heard loud shouts and saw the boys from Chi-Won's class. They were marching and Chi-Won was in the first row. The parade stopped. Some of the boys got into a **formation** that looked like they were going to do gymnastics. One held a square piece of wood above his head. Another stood with his head bowed. Chi-Won knelt on the ground with his head tucked under and his back held high. Suddenly a boy ran, jumped onto Chi-Won's back, then onto the shoulders of the other boy. He hurled himself into the air, feet first. He shouted "Hiyuh" and kicked the board held by the third boy. It split and fell to the ground.

**formation: line-up**

The jumper landed on his feet and bowed. Chi-Won and the other boys bowed, too. Everyone watching them cheered and clapped.

"Is that karate?" I asked.

"It's like karate, but it's called Tae Kwon Do," Mrs. Chung said.

There were more floats and high school bands and decorated cars. A man with a pushcart was selling Korean and American flags. I bought a Korean flag to take to school. I asked Mrs. Chung the meaning of the design in the center of the flag.

"The blue and red design in the circle is an ancient symbol of the universe. It stands for balance and **harmony** and also for opposites, like day and night, heat and cold."

harmony: peace; calm

There were sets of black bars in the corners of the flag. I asked what they meant.

"They're also ancient symbols. They stand for heaven, earth, fire, and water," Mrs. Chung explained. "Most Korean families have Korean and American flags. We're proud of both countries." I began to see what Mee-Yung meant when she said we'd get a lot of ideas for our report from the Harvest Festival. . . .

After the last float passed, we went to the park. Mrs. Chung went to meet Mee-Yung and Alina. There were stands selling Korean food. I bought something that looked like a pancake. The old man making the pancakes pointed to a red sauce and asked if I wanted some. I said I'd try it. When I took a bite of the pancake, I felt like my mouth was on fire. I fanned it with my hand.

Mee-Yung and Alina and their mother found me. Mrs. Chung laughed when I told her about the hot sauce. "Red peppers!" she said. "Why don't you come over to our house for dinner on Monday? I'll fix you some Korean food you'll like." She bought us all some cold punch. That cooled my mouth.

*Bonnie learns other customs from Mee-Yung and her family, such as taking your shoes off when you enter a house and eating with chopsticks. She tastes Korean food, listens to Korean music, and plays Korean games. She also learns about important celebrations, such as a child's first birthday and Korean New Year's Day. On report day, Bonnie and Mee-Yung dress up in hanbok and share all of these customs with their class. Suppose your class decided to have a "Salad Bowl" project. What customs would you want to learn about? What customs would you share?*

Source: Dianne MacMillan and Dorothy Freeman, *My Best Friend, Mee-Yung Kim*. Englewood Cliffs, NJ: Julian Messner, 1989.

# Music, Music for Everyone

## by Vera B. Williams

*People in a community get together to celebrate holidays, birthdays, and other special days. Music is often an important custom at these celebrations. People can have lots of fun singing and dancing and clapping to music. In this story Rosa and her friends form a band and provide the entertainment for a very special neighborhood party. As you read, notice all the different ways people help each other. How do you think working together brings people closer and helps to make things happen?*

Our big chair often sits in our living room empty now. When I first got my accordion, Grandma and Mama used to sit in that chair together to listen to me practice. And every day after school while Mama was at her job at the diner, Grandma would be sitting in the chair by the window. Even if it was snowing big flakes down on her hair, she would lean way out to call, "Hurry up, Pussycat. I've got something nice for you."

But now Grandma is sick. She has to stay upstairs in the big bed in Aunt Ida and Uncle Sandy's extra room. Mama and Aunt Ida and Uncle Sandy and I take turns taking care of her. When I come home from school, I run right upstairs to ask Grandma if she wants anything. I carry up the soup Mama has left for her. I water her plants and report if the **Christmas cactu**s has any flowers yet. Then I sit on her bed and tell her about everything.

**Christmas cactus:** a cactus that blooms every winter

Grandma likes it when my friends Leora, Jenny, and Mae come home with me because we play music for her. Leora plays the drums. Mae plays the flute. Jenny plays fiddle and I play my accordion. One time we played a dance for Grandma that we learned in the music club at school.

Grandma clapped until it made her too tired. She told us it was like the music in the village where she lived when she was a girl. It made her want to dance right down the street. We had to keep her from trying to hop out of bed to go to the kitchen to fix us a treat.

Leora and Jenny and Mae and I left Grandma to rest and went down to get our own treat. We squeezed together into our big chair to eat it.

"It feels sad down here without your grandma," Leora said. "Even your big money jar up there looks sad and empty."

"Remember how it was full to the top and I couldn't even lift it when we bought the chair for my mother?" I said.

"And remember how it was more than half full when you got your accordion?" Jenny said.

"I bet it's empty now because your mother has to spend all her money to take care of your grandma till she gets better. That's how it was when my father had his accident and couldn't go to work for a long time," Mae said.

Mae had a dime in her pocket and she dropped it into the jar. "That will make it look a little fuller anyway," she said as she went home.

But after Jenny and Leora and Mae went home, our jar looked even emptier to me. I wondered how we would ever be able to fill it up again while Grandma was sick. I wondered when Grandma would be able to come downstairs again. Even our beautiful chair with roses all over it seemed empty with just me in the corner of it. The whole house seemed so empty and so quiet.

I got out my accordion and I started to play. The notes sounded beautiful in the empty room. One song that is an old tune sounded so pretty I played it over and over. I remembered what my mother had told me about my other grandma and how she used to play the accordion. Even when she was a girl not much bigger than I, she would get up and play at a party or a wedding so the company could dance and sing. Then people would stamp their feet and yell, "More, more!" When they went home, they would leave money on the table for her.

That's how I got my idea for how I could help fill up the jar again. I ran right upstairs. "Grandma," I whispered. "Grandma?"

"Is that you, Pussycat?" she answered in a sleepy voice. "I was just having such a nice dream about you. Then I woke up and heard you playing that beautiful old song. Come. Sit here and brush my hair."

I brushed Grandma's hair and told her my whole idea. She thought it was a great idea. "But tell the truth, Grandma," I begged her. "Do you think kids could really do that?"

"I think you and Jenny and Leora and Mae could do it. No question. No question at all," she answered.

"Only don't wait a minute to talk to them about it. Go call and ask them now."

And that was how the Oak Street Band got started.

Our music teachers helped us pick out pieces we could all play together. Aunt Ida, who plays guitar, helped us practice. We practiced on our back porch. One day our neighbor leaned out his window in his pajamas and yelled, "Listen, kids, you sound great but give me a break. I work at night. I've got to get some sleep in the daytime." After that we practiced inside. Grandma said it was helping her get better faster than anything.

At last my accordion teacher said we sounded very good. Uncle Sandy said so too. Aunt Ida and Grandma said we were terrific. Mama said she thought anyone would be glad to have us play for them.

It was Leora's mother who gave us our first job. She asked us to come and play at a party for Leora's great-grandmother and great-grandfather. It was going to be a special **anniversary** for them. It was fifty years ago on that day they first opened their market on our corner. Now Leora's mother takes care of the market. She always plays the radio loud while she works. But for the party she said there just had to be live music.

**anniversary:** yearly celebration

All of Leora's aunts and uncles and cousins came to the party. Lots of people from our block came too. Mama and Aunt Ida and Uncle Sandy walked down from our house very slowly with Grandma. It was Grandma's first big day out.

There was a long table in the backyard made from little tables all pushed together. It was covered with so many big dishes of food you could hardly see the tablecloth. But I was too excited to eat anything.

Leora and Jenny and Mae and I waited over by the rosebush. Each of us had her instrument all ready. But everyone else went on eating and talking and eating some more. We didn't see how they would ever get around to listening to us. And we didn't see how we could be brave enough to begin.

At last Leora's mother pulled us right up in front of everybody. She banged on a pitcher with a spoon to get attention.

Then she introduced each one of us. "And *now* we're going to have music," she said. "Music and dancing for everyone."

It was quiet as school assembly. Every single person there was looking right at Leora and Jenny and Mae and me. But we just stood there and stared right back.

Then I heard my grandma whisper, "Play Pussycat. Play anything. Just like you used to play for me."

I put my fingers on the keys and buttons of my accordion. Jenny tucked her fiddle under her chin. Mae put her flute to her mouth. Leora held up her drums. After that we played and played. We made mistakes, but we played like a real band. The little lanterns came on. Everyone danced.

Mama and Aunt Ida and Uncle Sandy smiled at us every time they danced by. Grandma kept time nodding her head and tapping with the cane she uses now. Leora and Jenny and Mae and I forgot about being scared. We loved the sound of the Oak Street Band.

And afterward everybody clapped and shouted. Leora's great-grandfather and great-grandmother thanked us. They said we had made their party something they would always remember. Leora's father piled up plates of food for us. My mamma arranged for Leora, Jenny, and Mae to stay over at our house. And when we finally all went out the gate together, late at night, Leora's mother tucked an envelope with our money into Leora's pocket.

As soon as we got home, we piled into my bed to divide the money. We made four equal shares. Leora said she was going to save up for a bigger drum. Mae wasn't sure what she would do with her share. Jenny fell asleep before she could tell us. But I couldn't even lie down until I climbed up and put mine right into our big jar on the shelf near our chair.

*Vera Williams painted the pictures that go with this story. To see more of her artwork, check the book out from your library.*

Source: Vera B. Williams, *Music, Music for Everyone*. New York: Greenwillow, 1984.

# Mr. Griggs' Work

## by Cynthia Rylant

*Take a walk around your community. You might find a firehouse, a police station, a school, and a library. All of these places provide services to the people in your community. One of the most important services is provided by the United States government and can be found in even the smallest towns. This service is the post office! In the story below, Mr. Griggs runs a small post office. As you read the story, think about how Mr. Griggs serves the people in his community. How does he feel about his job?*

**M**r. Griggs worked at the old post office. He was pretty old himself.

He had spent millions of minutes of his long life **shuffling** through letters, watching the pictures on the stamps change, punching his First Class **puncher**, weighing fat brown boxes, and listening to long tales about "The Letter That Never Got There."

Mr. Griggs loved his job.

He thought about it almost all the time.

**shuffling:** sorting

**puncher:** rubber stamp that marks letters "First Class"

Now and then Mr. Griggs would be washing up his supper dishes when he'd start thinking about the fruitcake Mrs. McTacket had sent her sister fifteen Christmases ago.

That fruitcake had never arrived, and in the middle of his dishes Mr. Griggs would wonder, Where is that fruitcake?

Some nights he'd lie in bed wondering how much it would cost to mail a one-pound package to **New Zealand** or a three-ounce letter to **Taiwan**. It was hard not to get up in the middle of the night and go find out. And at times, he just couldn't help himself.

Even when he went for a quiet walk in the woods, Mr. Griggs couldn't stop thinking about his work.

When a bluejay zipped over his head, he'd think: "Express Mail."

When a squirrel darted up a tree with an acorn in its mouth, he'd think: "Special Delivery."

The little holes in a rotten maple tree would remind him of his mailboxes.

He couldn't even look at a chipmunk without remembering the chipmunk stamp of 1978. But Mr. Griggs didn't mind. He loved his work.

One day Mr. Griggs became sick. His head ached and his stomach hurt and he lay in bed all day long. It was the first time he'd ever been too sick to go to work, and now someone else was taking care of his post office. Someone else was sorting through Mr. Griggs' letters, someone else was putting pennies and nickels in Mr. Griggs' drawer, someone else was taping up the corners of one of Mr. Griggs' **ragged parcels.** Someone else was doing Mr. Griggs' work. Poor old Mr. Griggs felt like a **dead letter**.

But the next day his headache was gone and his stomach was better.

He was still tired, though, and because he was moving slower than usual he was a little late leaving for work.

New Zealand: a country in the Pacific Ocean

Taiwan: a country in Asia

**ragged parcels:** torn packages

**dead letter:** a letter that cannot be delivered

When he finally showed up at the old building, in front of it stood Mrs. Emma Bradshaw (Box 98), Mr. Frank Shrewsberry and his son Junior (Box 171), Miss Sue Ann Huckabee (Box 10), and young Bobby Bricker (Box 21).

Mr. Griggs was so glad to be back that he shook hands with them all and nearly squeezed the **dickens** out of young Bobby.

**dickens:** breath

Then he unlocked the door of his beloved post office. He settled himself behind his little window and to Miss Huckabee, who was first in line, he said, almost **gleefully,** "First Class or Parcel Post?"

He ran his fingers over his old letter scale, he sniffed at his stamp drawer, he lined up his **meters** and punchers, and he glanced lovingly at all the brass mailboxes lining the walls.

In all the world that day there was nothing finer than Mr. Griggs' work.

*The people who lived in Mr. Griggs' town were very lucky to have someone like him to run their post office. What made Mr. Griggs so special? Do you know people who care a lot about their work? How might their work help people in your community?*

Source: Cynthia Rylant, *Mr. Griggs' Work.* New York: Orchard Books, 1989.

# JOHN HENRY

### by Ezra Jack Keats

*When the United States was young, there were big jobs to do, and it took big people to do them. One of those big jobs was building a railroad. Tracks had to be put down over rivers, through mountains, and across deserts and plains. The biggest man to do this was John Henry. Some folks say he was born with a hammer in his hand. The story of how he drove the steel spikes, or heavy nails, into the ground to lay our country's railroad tracks has been handed down from generation to generation. Like the story of Paul Bunyan, it is a tall tale. What parts of the story of John Henry do you think could be true?*

"Bang! Bang! Bang!" rang little John Henry's hammer through the cabin, as he crawled about. "What's that **rascal** up to now?" his mother chuckled. And before she knew it, he was big enough to help her around the house. As he grew up, he did a man's work with his father. One day John Henry thought, "I'm taller and stronger than anyone around. It's time I went out into the world." He said goodbye to his mother and father, and off he went. He worked on farms and in cotton fields, but all that was too **tame**. So he got himself a job on a riverboat.

One stormy night the ship **plowed** through the darkness. Suddenly the big steel rod that turned the paddle wheel broke. The wheel stopped turning. Smash! went the rod through the bottom of the ship. "Pump water!" shouted the captain. "Get to **port** before we sink!" John Henry leaped to the paddle-wheel crank. He **seized** it, pushed and grunted and pulled. Slowly the giant wheel turned. With all his strength he kept it turning. "Lord Almighty, help us," someone

**rascal:** a playful person

**tame:** not exciting

**plowed:** moved forward

**port:** place along shore where boats can anchor

**seized:** grabbed

whispered in that long, dark night. As day broke, they sighted shore and pulled into port. A thunderous cheer went up for John Henry!

John Henry felt a new excitement in the air. Men were talking of railroads being built from the Atlantic to the Pacific. "They're goin' to lay those tracks over rivers, across prairies and deserts, and right through the mountains."

"And through Indian lands and stampeding buffalo herds, and **badlands**." "Goodbye, boys," cried John Henry. "I'm goin' to swing me a hammer on them beautiful new tracks!"

**badlands:** a region with little plant life

"My hands are just itchin' to hold a hammer again," John Henry said. He tried one for size, and laughed. "It sure does feel fine."

How he drove those spikes, singing to the clanging of his hammer! The men joined in, their voices singing, hammers ringing. And John Henry's gang was in the lead as day after day the tracks moved steadily westward.

Rising across their path was a **sprawling** mountain range. Its snow-capped peaks reached high into the clouds. "We'll have to tunnel through," said his friend, L'il Bill. "It'll be awful dangerous. Could be cave-ins," someone put in. "That suits me fine," said John Henry.

**sprawling:** spread out

"Me, too," added L'il Bill.

"Here's how we'll do it, boys," the **foreman** called out. "A couple of men'll drive a hole into the rock. Then the powder men'll put dynamite into the hole and explode it. The others'll cart the loose rock away. We'll do this again and again until we have a tunnel right through this mountain. And it's goin' to be a real big tunnel, boys. Big enough for a giant locomotive pullin' one o' them long strings o' trains. All right, boys, **blast** away!"

**foreman:** a person in charge of a group of workers

**blast:** blow up

Deep into the mountain they worked, as John Henry's singing echoed through the tunnel. The powder men got ready to blast more rock. They filled a hole with dynamite, put in a long **fuse**, and lit it. "Run, men!" cried the foreman.

**fuse:** a cord that is lit to set off dynamite

They all scrambled back, ready to dash clear of the blast. At that instant came a great cracking and rumbling and the entire tunnel trembled around them.

"It's a cave-in!" "We're trapped!"

There was no place to run. The fuse burned closer to the dynamite. John Henry was nearest the fuse. He ran to put it out but tripped and fell!

"Oooh, I'm hurt bad," he groaned. "I can't get up." The fuse burned farther out of reach. Others rushed toward it, but they were too far away. Suddenly John Henry remembered—he still had his hammer in his hand! Down came the hammer. Smack! on the burning tip. The fuse was out, danger past. Sighs of relief filled the smoky tunnel.

"Whew! Help me up, boys," mumbled John Henry. Clearing their way through the cave-in, the men carried him to safety. Some days later they heard an unfamiliar clatter. Down the tunnel came a group of men with a strange machine. "This is a steam drill. It can drill more holes faster than any six men combined," a new man bragged. "Who can beat that?"

John Henry stepped forward. "Try me!" He and L'il Bill took their work places. John Henry gripped his hammer. L'il Bill clutched his steel drill. "Check the machine," came an order. A nervous hand fell on the switch. In the dark both sides waited for the signal to start. A hoarse voice counted, "One, two—THREE!"

The machine shrieked as it started. John Henry swung his hammer—and a crash of steel on steel split the air! Clang! Bang! Clang! The drill got red-hot in L'il Bill's hands. He quickly dropped it and picked up another. Hiss! Whistle! Rattle! Men **frantically heaved** coal into the hungry, roaring engine and poured water into the steaming **boiler.**

Whoop! Clang! Whoop! Bang!

John Henry's hammer whistled as he swung it.

Chug, chug! Clatter! rattled the machine.

Hour after hour raced by. The machine was ahead!

**frantically:** in an excited, worried way

**heaved:** threw

**boiler:** a large container in which water is changed into steam for running an engine

"Hand me that twenty-pound hammer, L'il Bill!"
Harder and faster crashed the hammer. Great chunks
of rock fell as John Henry ripped hole after hole into
the tunnel wall. The machine rattled and whistled and
drilled even faster. Friends **doused** John Henry and L'il
Bill with cold water to keep them going. . . .

**doused:** soaked

John Henry swung both mighty hammers—faster
and faster. He moved so fast the men could see only a
blur and sparks from his striking hammers. His strokes
rang out like great heart-beats. At the other side of the
tunnel the machine shrieked, groaned and rattled, and
drilled. Then all at once it shook and shuddered—
wheezed—and stopped. Frantically men worked to get
it going again. But they couldn't. It had **collapsed!**

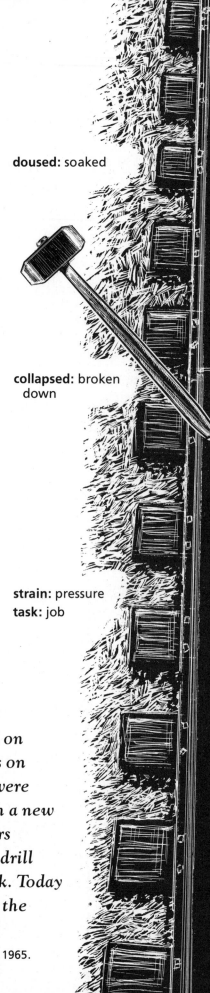

**collapsed:** broken
down

John Henry's hammering still rang and echoed
through the tunnel with a strong and steady beat.
Suddenly there was a great crash. Light streamed into
the dark tunnel. John Henry had broken through!
Wild cries of joy burst from the men. Still holding one
of his hammers, John Henry stepped out into the
glowing light of a dying day. It was the last step he ever
took. Even the great heart of John Henry could not
bear the **strain** of his last **task**. John Henry died with
his hammer in his hand.

**strain:** pressure
**task:** job

If you listen to the locomotives roaring through the
tunnels and across the land, you'll hear them singing—
singing of that great steel-driving man—John Henry.
Listen!

*There really was a John Henry, and this story is based on*
*something that really happened. In the 1870s workers on*
*the Chesapeake and Ohio Railroad in West Virginia were*
*building the Big Bend Tunnel. A man came along with a new*
*steam drill and said it could dig faster than the workers*
*using hammers. The real John Henry raced the steam drill*
*and won. He died when he was crushed by falling rock. Today*
*John Henry is a folk hero. He helps us remember that the*
*United States was built by people, not machines.*

Source: Ezra Jack Keats, *John Henry: An American Legend*. New York: Knopf, 1965.

# Where the River Begins

## by Thomas Locker

*When water flows from one place to another, a river is formed. Rivers flow into larger rivers or into other bodies of water, such as lakes and oceans. But where do rivers begin? In this story, two boys try to find out where the river that runs past their house begins. Join them on this exciting journey into the mountains. As you read, notice the different ways the author describes the river. How does the river change as the boys get closer to where it begins?*

**O**nce there were two boys named Josh and Aaron who lived with their family in a big yellow house. Nearby was a river that flowed gently into the sea. On summer evenings the boys liked to sit on their porch watching the river and making up stories about it. Where, they wondered, did the river begin.

Their grandfather loved the river and had lived near it all his life. Perhaps he would know. One day

Josh and Aaron asked their grandfather to take them on a camping trip to find the beginning of the river. When he agreed, they made plans and began to pack. They started out early the next morning. For a time they walked along a familiar road past fields of golden wheat and sheep grazing in the sun. Nearby flowed the river—gentle, wide, and deep.

At last they reached the **foothills** of the mountains. The road had ended and now the river would be their only guide. It raced over rocks and **boulders** and had become so narrow that the boys and their grandfather could jump across.

**foothills:** low hills at the bottom of a mountain

**boulders:** large rocks

In the late afternoon, while the sun was still hot, the river led them into a dark forest. They found a **campsite** and set up their tent. Then the boys went wading in the cold river water.

**campsite:** place to camp

The first long day away from home was over. That night, around the flickering campfire, their grandfather told Josh and Aaron stories. Drifting off to sleep, they listened to the forest noises and were **soothed** by the sound of the river.

**soothed:** calmed

**Dawn** seemed to come quickly and the sun glowed through a thick mist. The boys were eager to be off, but their grandfather was stiff from sleeping on the ground and was slower getting started.

**dawn:** the beginning of day.

The path they chose led them high above the river. On a grassy **knoll** they stopped to gaze around. The morning mist had risen and formed white clouds in the sky. In the distance the river **meandered** lazily. It was so narrow that it seemed almost to disappear. They all felt a great excitement, for they knew they were nearing the end of their journey.

**knoll:** small, round hill

**meandered:** followed a winding course

Without a word the boys began to run. They followed the river for an hour or more until it **trickled** into a still pond, high in an **upland** meadow. In this small, peaceful place the river began. Finally their search was over. As they started back, the sky suddenly darkened.

**trickled:** flowed slowly

**upland:** high land

Thunder crashed around them and lightning lit the sky. They **pitched** their tent and crawled inside just before the storm broke. Rain pounded on the roof of their small tent all night long, but they were warm and dry inside.

**pitched:** set up

In the morning long before dawn they were awakened by a roaring, rushing sound. The river had **swelled** with the storm and was flooding its **banks**. They tried to take a shortcut across a field but were soon ankle deep in water. Grandfather explained that the river drew its waters from the rains high up in the mountains.

**swelled:** risen higher
**banks:** edges

They came down out of the foothills in the soft light of late afternoon. The boys recognized the cliffs along the river and knew they were close to home. Their **weariness** lifted and they began to move more quickly down the road.

**weariness:** tired feeling

At last they reached their house on the hill. The boys raced ahead to tell their mother and father about the place where the river began. But their grandfather paused for a moment and in the fading light he watched the river, which continued on as it always had, flowing gently into the sea.

*As you read this story, could you imagine the river when it was gentle and wide, or fast and narrow? Could you picture a lazy, winding river, or a roaring, rushing one? What are some other things in nature that change?*

Source: Thomas Locker, *Where the River Begins.* New York: Dial, 1984.

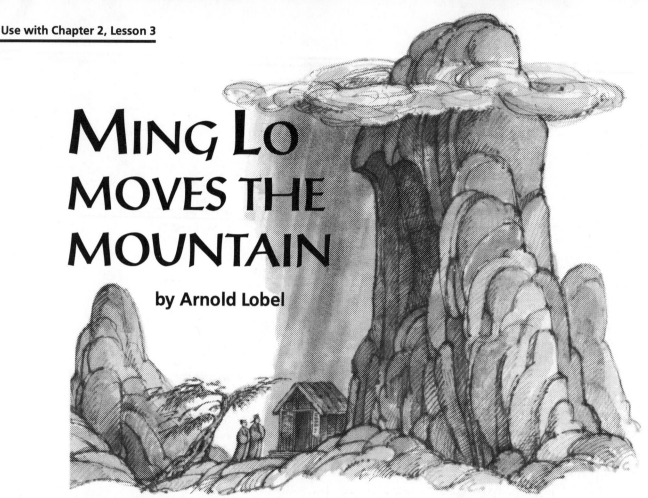

# MING LO MOVES THE MOUNTAIN

## by Arnold Lobel

*The landforms around you make a difference in the way you live. Can you imagine what it would be like to live right at the bottom of a large mountain? Just ask Ming Lo and his wife, the characters in this story about a Chinese couple. To them, the mountain is a big problem. But how do you move a mountain? Read the story to find out the clever way that they solve their problem.*

Ming Lo and his wife lived in a house at the bottom of a large mountain. They loved their house, but they did not love the mountain.

Rocks and stones broke loose from the cliffs. They dropped down onto the house of Ming Lo. The roof was full of holes. Clouds formed on the top of the mountain. Heavy rain fell from the clouds onto this roof that was full of holes. The rooms inside were damp and drippy.

When the sun did shine, it never warmed the house of Ming Lo. The mountain always cast a dark shadow. The flowers and vegetables in the garden grew thin and **sparse**.     **sparse:** widely apart

"This mountain brings us nothing but unhappiness," said the wife of Ming Lo. "Husband, you must move the mountain so that we may enjoy our house in peace."

"My dear wife," said Ming Lo, "how can one small man such as I move a large mountain such as this?"

"How should I know?" said his wife. "There is a wise man who lives in the village. Go and ask him."

Ming Lo hurried to the village. When he found the wise man, he said, "I want to move the mountain that is near my house."

The wise man thought for a long time. . . .

Finally he said, "Go home, Ming Lo. Cut down the tallest, thickest tree you can find. Push this tree against the side of the mountain with all your strength. This is the way that you will move the mountain."

Ming Lo ran home. He cut down the tallest, thickest tree that he could find. Ming Lo and his wife held tightly to the tree. Running as fast as they could run, they pushed the tree against the side of the mountain.

The tree split in half. Ming Lo and his wife fell on their heads. The mountain did not move an inch.

"Go back to the wise man," said the wife of Ming Lo.

"Ask him to think of another way to move the mountain."

Again the wise man thought for a long time. . . .

Finally he said, "Go home, Ming Lo. Take the pots and pans from your kitchen. Hold a spoon in each one of your hands. With these spoons, hit the pots and pans as hard as you can. Raise your voice in loud shouts and cries. The mountain will be frightened by the noise. This is the way that you will move the mountain."

Ming Lo ran home. He took the pots and pans from his kitchen. Ming Lo and his wife held a spoon in each one of their four hands. They shouted and cried. They hit the pots and pans as hard as they could.

They made a great noise. Flocks of birds flew out of the trees, but the mountain did not move at all.

"Go back to the wise man," cried the wife of Ming Lo. "We must find a way to move the mountain."

Ming Lo watched as the wise man thought for a very long time. . . .

Finally he said, "Go home, Ming Lo. Bake many cakes and loaves of bread. Bring these to the spirit who lives at the top of the mountain. The spirit is always hungry. He will be happy to receive your gifts. He will grant your every wish. This is the way that you will move the mountain."

Ming Lo ran home. With his wife, he baked platters of cakes and baskets of bread. Together they began the steep climb to the top of the mountain where the spirit lived.

They felt a strong wind as they struggled up the high cliffs. It whistled and howled.

Soon the air was filled with flying cakes and loaves of bread. There was nothing left for the spirit and the mountain did not move.

Without waiting for his wife to say a word, Ming Lo went quickly back to the wise man.

"Help me to move this mountain so that I may enjoy my house in peace!" cried Ming Lo.

The wise man sat in deep thought for a long, long time. . . .

Finally he said, "Go home, Ming Lo. Take your house apart, stick by stick. Gather all these sticks that are the pieces of your house. Collect all of the things that are your **possessions**. **Bind** everything into bundles with rope and **twine**. Carry these bundles in your arms and on the top of your head. Face the mountain and close your eyes.

"Having done all this," said the wise man, "you will step to the dance of the moving mountain. You will put your left foot in a place that is in back of your right foot. Then you will put your right foot in a place that is in back of your left foot. You must do this again

**possessions:** belongings
**bind:** tie
**twine:** strong cord

30

and again for many hours. When you open your eyes,
you will see that the mountain has moved far away."

"This is a strange dance," said Ming Lo, "but if it
makes the mountain move, I will do it at once."

Ming Lo ran home. He took his house apart, stick
by stick. He gathered all of the sticks and collected all
of the things that were his possessions.

Ming Lo and his wife bound everything into
bundles with rope and twine. They carried the bundles
in their arms and on the tops of their heads.

Then Ming Lo showed his wife how to do the
dance of the moving mountain. They faced the
mountain and closed their eyes. Carefully, they began
to move their feet to the steps of the dance.

They each put their left foot in a place that was
behind their right foot. Then they each put their right
foot in a place that was behind their left foot.

The neighbors saw Ming Lo and his wife walking backward across the fields with all of their possessions.

It was an odd sight and they watched in wonder.

After many hours had passed, Ming Lo and his wife opened their eyes.

"Look," cried Ming Lo, "our dance has done its work! The mountain has moved far away!"

Stick by stick, they rebuilt their house. They unpacked all of their possessions and made themselves at home.

Ming Lo and his wife lived the rest of their lives under an open sky and a warm sun. When rain fell, it came down gently on a roof that had no holes.

They often looked at the mountain that was small in the distance. There was happiness in their hearts for they both knew that they had made the mountain move.

*Ming Lo and his wife could now live in peace and enjoy the beauty of the mountains in the distance. Did Ming Lo and his wife really make the mountain move? What does the story teach about living with nature?*

Source: Arnold Lobel, *Ming Lo Moves the Mountain*. New York: Greenwillow, 1982.

# OUR FIRST COMMUNITIES

*We can all be a little like the birds: they leave the earth with wings, and we can also leave the world by letting our thoughts rise as high as the birds fly.*

from *The Great Race*
by Paul Goble

# The Great Race

**Retold
by Paul Goble**

*At one time millions of buffalo roamed the Great Plains of North America. They were the most important source of food to the Indians who lived in this area. But Sioux and Cheyenne storytellers say that long, long ago it was the buffalo that ate people! Then the Creator held a Great Race to decide who should eat whom. In Paul Goble's retelling of the story, who wins the race?*

**D**o you know why buffaloes have long hair on their chins?

Long ago, when the world was still quite new, buffaloes used to eat people. It is true! The hair on their chins is hair of the people they used to eat. Ya-a-a-a. . . It is terrible to think about those times. . . .

The Creator saw how people suffered. He heard their prayers for help. There came a day when he told Crow to call all living things together to the hills which rise like an island from the center of the great plains. The people, and buffaloes, and every bird and animal heard Crow calling, and they came to the hills from all directions across the plains.

The Creator stood on the highest hilltop, and spoke to them all: "Toke. Is it right that buffaloes eat people? Or should people eat buffaloes instead? All you

tribes of **four-leggeds** and **wingeds** will
decide. There will be a race around these hills. If the
buffaloes win the race, they will still eat people. But
if the people win the race, they will eat the buffaloes
and all four-leggeds instead. Get ready. Choose your
fastest runners. Join the side you want to win."

The people chose a young man. He had never lost a
race. Even the buffaloes knew he would be hard to beat,
but they had a young cow to run for them. She was
everyone's favorite, and they were sure she would win.

The animals joined with the buffaloes, because they
have four legs. The birds sided with the people, because
they have two legs, as we do. Each tribe chose its
fastest runner. Suddenly Wolf and Coyote raised their
heads and h-o-w-l-e-d. Ho po! The runners sped away
with a thunder of feet and a great wind of flying birds.

The birds flew ahead like arrows. **Magpie** beat her
wings fast, and even the tiniest birds left her behind.
But she had made up her mind she was going to win.
She had been thinking things out, and had made a
plan: she flew down and sat on Buffalo's back.

The day was hot. The birds were panting, and when
they came to a stream they stopped to drink. But they

drank too much, and then fell asleep in the trees. The animals swam past them; except for Beaver, whose legs were too short for such a long race, and he slipped into a lovely pool in the shade of the trees. Otter followed, and Muskrat too.

Buffalo and the young man took the lead, and the larger animals were staying close behind. Magpie had not made a sound; nobody had even noticed her sitting on Buffalo's back.

Jack-rabbit was hopping along well until he saw Coyote trotting up behind him; he was so frightened that he fled out onto the plains. He is still there, always wondering who is behind him.

Nobody remembers how long they raced around the hills; it was several days. Tired runners dropped out all along the way. Prairie Dog wasted his energy chattering at Hawk. Rattlesnake ate Toad and then curled up to sleep. Mouse vanished down a hole when Bear almost stepped on her. Mole and Gopher tunneled along underground, and they still think the race is on.

The young man fell farther and farther behind Buffalo. He had run his best. Nobody could say he would have run better. Even Buffalo was almost exhausted, and her head hung low. Magpie was still clinging to the thick woolly fur of Buffalo's back. But when Buffalo saw the finishing line, she ran faster in a final effort. All the four-legged animals watching from the hillsides cheered her. They were quite sure she was the winner. Suddenly Magpie flew up from Buffalo's back. Everyone had forgotten about her! She was feeling good and was not tired at all! Magpie flew up towards the sun. And then she swooped down, squawking and squawking, and crossed the finishing line just in front of Buffalo. A great shout of people and birds filled the air. Magpie, the slowest of all the birds, had won the race for the two-leggeds! Ho hecetu welo.

The chiefs of the Buffalo Nation told the people: "That was a fair race. Now we are under your power. You will eat us." And then the Creator spoke to the people: "Use your power wisely. Look after all things that I have made, even the smallest of them. They are all your relatives. Make yourselves worthy of them, and give thanks always."

After that the people were shown how to make bows and arrows, and they were given horses. They hunted the buffaloes when they needed meat.

Nobody ever harms Magpie. The people have always been grateful to the birds for taking their side in The Great Race. They honor them when they wear their beautiful feathers.

We can all be a little like the birds: they leave the earth with wings, and we can also leave the world by letting our thoughts rise as high as the birds fly.

It is also told that Magpie flew so near the sun, that the sun's **iridescent** colors are in her tail—and, in the night sky, what we know as the Milky Way, are the clouds of dust raised by the runners. The Great Race was the start of many things.

iridescent: shiny

*In keeping with this story, Indians killed the buffalo only when they needed meat and gave thanks after every hunt. There were so many buffalo it seemed that there would always be buffalo. But as white people came to the Great Plains, the buffalo herds got smaller. Hunters began killing buffalo by the millions, and by 1890 the buffalo herds were almost all gone. As a result, the Plains Indians had to change their way of life. Today, stories like* The Great Race *remind us of the Plains Indians' culture and of the time when America's largest animal roamed freely across the plains.*

Source: Paul Goble, *The Great Race*. New York: Bradbury, 1985.

# Before You Came This Way

## by Byrd Baylor

*Anasazi is an Indian word that means "ancient ones." The Anasazi Indians were one of the early groups who lived in the American Southwest. They built their homes out of stone, into the sides of mesas or cliffs. In this selection, author Byrd Baylor describes rock paintings that are found on the walls of these ancient homes. How do Baylor's descriptions help bring these paintings to life? How does this poem describe life in this area hundreds of years ago?*

You walk
down this canyon,
this place of
high red cliffs
and turning winds
and hawks that float
in a far white sky
and
you wonder:
"Am I the first one
ever
to come this way?"

And
you wonder
"Is my footprint
the first one
ever
to touch this sand?"

But
then you see something
which tells you,
No,
you're not the first.
Your brothers
out of some
long ago lost age
passed this way too.

You see their marks
on canyon walls.

Even the print
of their hands
is left,
chipped deep
in stone.

These men who came before you—
cliff dwellers,
hunters,
wanderers—
left messages
on rocks,
on cliff sides,
on steep rough
canyon walls.

They drew
the things
they did
and saw.
They even drew
their corn plants

and the birds
that flew above
their heads
and the paths

men cut
through nameless lands.

The reds
and yellows
and blacks
have been battered
by a thousand winds,
washed by a thousand rains.

The pictures are dim now,
half shadow,
but you search the canyon
for them.

And here
you see
young hunters
leap
in the morning sun.
The light still
gleams on their
arrows.

And here
a coyote
howls at the moon.

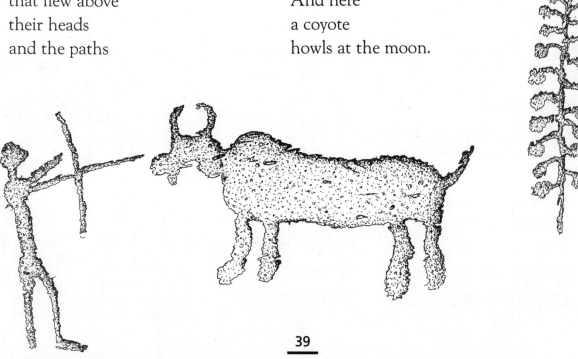

From his own hill
he guards his world.
He keeps the moon
in sight.

And rabbits flick
their ears
listening

listening

listening

while men do battle.
That fierce battle
raged
loud as thunder
across this canyon
Once

You find deer
with great antlers
branching like trees.

What is it they hear?

In the wind
there's the scent
of a mountain lion
who twitches his whiskers,
twitches his tail,
as he smiles
at himself. . .
or the deer.

Mountain goats
with curly horns.

Goats.
Goats.
More goats.
They drew them everywhere.
The clink of sharp hoofs
must have rung
as those goats jumped
from rock
to rock
to rock—

and then jumped back
where they had been
before. . . .

High on a rock
someone drew
tracks of all the birds
he'd ever seen
and deer tracks,
lion tracks,
fox tracks . . .
even a wandering path
of the tracks of
men.

Men going where?
Searching for a
better place
for the tribe
to make its home?
Or for some newer
hunting ground?

Did pictures bring
strength
to the hunters?

Did they bring luck?
Was there some
magic
in the artist's hand?

There must have been magic
in songs and dances too...
Songs to protect
hunters,
songs to make
children grow
and corn grow
and pumpkins.

People danced.

You ALMOST know
how it must have been.
Long lines of dancers
move
into the shadows.

You ALMOST hear
the chanting
and the flute
and the rattles
and the drums
that called down rain
and made the night winds
blow.

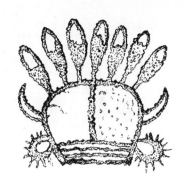

Sometimes
the dancers put on
masks.
Their artists drew
those great fierce faces
with headdresses
so tall and bright
and feathery
that they looked
part bird
part sky,
part mountain—
no longer men at all.

And
this canyon
echoed
with their voices.

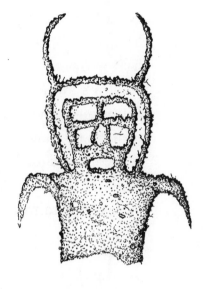

Did they ever
wonder
who
in some far later time
would stand
in their
canyon
and think of them
and ALMOST hear
the echo of those voices
still in the wind?

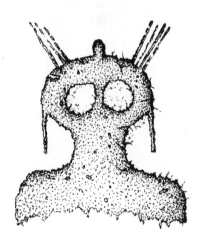

*Today you can see beautiful rock paintings of the Anasazi at Cliff Palace in Mesa Verde National Park in Colorado. Suppose you drew paintings to describe your life and your community. What pictures would you draw?*

Source: Byrd Baylor, *Before You Came This Way.* New York: Dutton, 1969.

# Why We Have Dogs in Hopi Villages

## told to Byrd Baylor by Hopi Indian children

*Byrd Baylor has lived in the Southwest all her life. She has written many books about the plants and animals of the desert and about the people living there, both today and long ago. You have already read one of Baylor's books, which appears on pages 38-41. Baylor also wrote the following story from her book And It Is Still That Way, but she did not write it by herself. Instead, she went to schools on Indian reservations in Arizona and asked children to share their favorite story from their Indian group. In that way, they could help pass on the customs and beliefs of their people. This story was written by a group of Hopi Indian children from the Second Mesa Day School. How do the dogs help the Hopi?*

There was a boy about our age. He lived in a Hopi village way up on the mesa. In those days the people were always arguing and fussing with each other and this boy used to say he was going to find some way to stop all that bad feeling.

He thought that if he went away and saw another village where people got along better he could come back and tell his people what to do and they would thank him.

He knew it would be a long journey. But all he took with him was a water jar and a loaf of bread that his mother baked for him.

When he went down the path that led away from his village he did not know which way to go. He just walked where he felt like going. Day after day he walked.

After many days had passed the boy came to the edge of a village he had never seen. It seemed like a happy place where people got along. But as he came closer he could see that it was a village of dogs, not people.

He asked the dogs if he could speak to their chief. Even though they had never seen a human before, they could tell that this boy came in peace so they let him enter their village.

They took him down the ladder into the kiva where **councils** and ceremonies are held. The dog chief sat with all his dog councilmen in a circle. The boy joined them in the circle. . . .

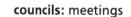 councils: meetings

Then it was time to speak. The boy said, "I came to get your help so the people of my village can find out how to stop arguing and fighting all the time. Maybe some of those dogs will go back with me."

But the chief said, "It will be up to my people. I will have no part in this."

They came out of the kiva together but none of the dogs offered to go with the boy. None of them wanted to leave his own village.

When night came the boy went to a little clearing outside the village and he lay awake for a long time trying to think of a way to get the dogs to go with him.

At last a spirit came down to him from the North Star.

"What do you want?" the spirit asked. "I have all the things that you could want."

The boy did not know what to ask for. But he remembered that many of the dogs looked thin and hungry so he said, "Some food would be good."

The spirit got the food and blessed it. When the boy awoke the food was there beside him. Some of the dogs ran up to the pile of food and began to eat it.

As soon as the boy saw that the dogs were eating the blessed food he knew he had asked the spirit for the right thing. He knew he had found a way to make the dogs follow him.

He went down into the kiva again with the dog leaders of that village. . . . Then the boy told the chief, "Some of the dogs ate my food. Those are the dogs that will be willing to go with me. They belong to me now because they took my food."

It was true.

The dogs that had eaten the blessed food gathered around the boy wherever he stood. They followed him all the way to his own village up on the mesa.

He gave one dog to each family. The people were so happy to have the dogs that they stopped quarreling.

Hopi villages have been peaceful ever since.

Now dogs have their jobs here. They guard our houses and our people and go to the fields with us and watch over the sheep. And they still remind us not to quarrel. That is their main job.

*Did you notice the way this story ended? Indian storytellers like to link the past with the present. This helps to keep the old ways alive and shows the importance of the past to life today. That is why Indian storytellers often end their stories with something like "And it is still that way."*

Source: Byrd Baylor, *And It Is Still That Way*. New York: Scribner's, 1976.

# Cross and Sword

## by Paul Green

*In 1965, St. Augustine Florida, celebrated its 400th birthday. As part of the celebration, a writer named Paul Green wrote a play about St. Augustine's early days called Cross and Sword. Its characters include Pedro Menéndez de Aviles—the founder of St. Augustine, Florida—one of the city's leading priests, and a group of Spanish settlers. The following is part of the last scene of the play. How does the play help bring history to life?*

**Act II Scene 6**

NARRATOR: It is the spring of 1567 in St. Augustine, Florida. For two years Pedro Menéndez de Avilés has been working to found the colony of St. Augustine for Spain. In that time, the colony has faced diseases, a lack of food, and even a hurricane. The colonists and the Native Americans have fought terrible battles for land and food.

Finally, the colony seems safe. Menéndez is about to return to Spain to bring back food, supplies and more Spanish people to live in St. Augustine.

\* \* \* \* \*

FATHER LOPEZ: When we landed here less than two years ago we prayed that the blessings of God would stay with us. And so they have, and St. Augustine is safe and **thriving**. Let us say our thanks unto God.

thriving: doing very well

45

**SPANISH SETTLERS:** Thanks be unto God.

**MENÉNDEZ:** Yes, our city lives! And let us at this hour remember our Indian brothers who have suffered at our hands. And so we shall try to repay them with service and kindness to them. And now, farewell. Be loyal to the new governor!

*(The crowd cheers!)*

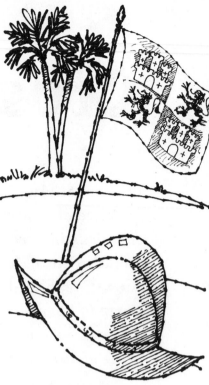

**MENÉNDEZ:** Soon I shall return again from Spain with more people and supplies. And whatever happens—even if this fort fell down, the **missions** rotted, the bells dropped unheard, and no piece of our work remained—still the glory of our struggles would not die. So, brothers, my friends, let us continue of strong heart and long patience! Once more, farewell. God be with you.

**missions:** religious settlements or buildings

**SPANISH SETTLERS:** God be with you, Your **Excellency**.

**excellency:** title of honor

*(Menéndez starts to leave. The Spanish settlers are now waving handkerchiefs and flags toward the departing Menéndez.)*

**MENÉNDEZ:** **Viva** St. Augustine!!

**viva:** Spanish word for "long live"

**CROWD:** Viva! Viva! Viva St. Augustine!

*Today this play is performed every night in an outdoor theater in St. Augustine. In 1973 the Florida government named* Cross and Sword *"Florida's Official State Play." If you were to write a play for your state or community, what would it be about?*

Source: Paul Green, *Cross and Sword.* New York: Samuel French Inc., 1965.

# . . . If You Sailed on the
# MAYFLOWER

## by Ann McGovern

*Look in any social studies or history book and you can find out certain facts about the Pilgrims. For example, they sailed from England on the Mayflower. The ship carried 102 passengers and arrived in America in 1620. But what was life on the Mayflower like? Where did people sleep and what did they eat? And what did the children on the Mayflower do for fun? Ann McGovern has researched these questions and has written a book giving the answers. In what ways does sailing on the Mayflower sound difficult? In what ways does it sound exciting?*

*How many people sailed on the* Mayflower?

Too many people!

The *Mayflower* carried about thirty sailors and one hundred and two passengers. Thirty-four of them were children.

There were not supposed to be that many people on the *Mayflower*. Some passengers were supposed to sail . . . on the smaller ship, the *Speedwell*, but something went wrong.

The two ships had begun their voyage from England together on August 5, 1620. But the *Speedwell* was leaky and had to go back to shore.

Some of the passengers from the *Speedwell* stayed behind in England. Others crowded onto the *Mayflower*. . . .

A baby boy was born as the *Mayflower* sailed across the Atlantic Ocean. Guess what his parents named him. *Oceanus!*

*What would you eat and drink on the* Mayflower?

Day after day, you would eat the same kind of food. You would not like it the first day, and by the last day you would be sick and tired of it.

Most of the time you would eat *salt horse* and *hardtack*. That's what the sailors called it.

Salt horse was their name for salted beef or pork or fish.

Hardtack was a hard, dry biscuit.

There were dried peas and beans, cheese from Holland, and some butter.

To cook their food, the Pilgrims would have had to build charcoal fires in metal boxes called *braziers*. But most of the time the weather was so stormy that it was too dangerous to have a fire. So most of the time the Pilgrims ate cold food. . . .

*Would you have had any fun on the* Mayflower?

It might be fun to watch the sailors. And you could play with the dogs. There were at least two dogs on board.

And there was a cat. Every ship had a cat to catch the rats.

There were plenty of books to read—if you liked grownup books. One of the Pilgrim leaders, William Brewster, brought along many books.

If you liked to sing, you would have fun singing. The Pilgrims sang Psalms—religious songs—every day.

*Would you get into trouble on the* Mayflower?

If you were like John and Francis Billington, you would.

The Billington boys were always getting into trouble.

One day, Francis Billington set fire to a piece of rope. He was standing close to some barrels of gunpowder.

If just one spark from the rope had gone into the gunpowder—BOOM! You would not be reading this book. For that would have been the end of the *Mayflower*, the end of the Pilgrims, and the end of our story.

The Pilgrims said it was God's mercy that saved them that day.

*When did the Pilgrims first see land?*

It was the morning of November 9, 1620. The Pilgrims saw a sandy beach. They saw trees and bushes.

They had reached Cape Cod, in what is today the state of Massachusetts. Now there is a town—Provincetown—at the very place the Pilgrims landed.

The voyage took sixty-six days—counting from September 6, the day the *Mayflower* left the *Speedwell* behind and sailed from Plymouth, England.

*What happened to the* Mayflower?

On April 5, 1621, almost four months after landing at Plymouth, Captain Jones and his crew sailed the *Mayflower* back to England.

Captain Jones said he would take any of the Pilgrims who wanted to go back with him. But not one Pilgrim went back.

The Pilgrims had been through terrible times. They would stay together now—no matter what might happen.

**The first winter in America was very hard for the Pilgrims. More than half of them died. But more kept coming, and with the help of local Indians, the Pilgrims survived. Do you have questions about life on the Mayflower or about early Pilgrim life? If you do, you can probably find the answers by reading the rest of Ann McGovern's . . . If You Sailed on the Mayflower. Look for the book in your school or town library.**

Source: Ann McGovern, . . . *If You Sailed on the Mayflower.* New York: Four Winds, 1969.

# In Good Old Colony Times

## American Ballad

*After the sun had set and the day's work was over, the Pilgrims often sang songs to entertain themselves. Many sang ballads, or songs that tell a story. These songs were passed along from town to town. Later they were written down and published. The ballad below was one of the first famous ballads in the American colonies. Why do the miller, the weaver, and the tailor fall into trouble?*

*Words adapted by Phyllis R. Kaplan*

1. In good old col-on-y times,___ when we lived un-der the king,___
2. O the first he was___ a mil-ler, and the second he was___ a wea-ver,

Three___ rogu-ish chaps fell in-to mis-haps, be-cause they could not sing,___
And the third he was a tail-or man, Three rogu-ish chaps to-ge-ther.

**Refrain**

Be-cause they could not sing, Be-cause they could not sing,

Three___ rogu-ish chaps fell in-to mis-haps, be-cause they could not sing.

3. O the miller, he stole corn;
   and the weaver, he stole yarn,
   And the tailor man ran right away
   with the broadcloth under his arm.

4. The miller was drowned in the dam,
   and the weaver got hung in his yarn,
   And the tailor tripped as he ran away
   with the broadcloth under his arm.

# TYPES OF COMMUNITIES

*Sing a song of people
Who like to come and go;
Sing of city people
You see but never know!*

from "Sing a Song of People"
by Lois Lenski

# The Best Town in the World

## by Byrd Baylor

*There are thousands of small towns in the United States. Each one is different and each is special in its own way. In this selection, Byrd Baylor tells about the town her father grew up in. It's in a rural part of Texas, surrounded by ranches and farms. Maybe it's just "a little, dirt-road, one-store, country town," but to Byrd Baylor's father it's the best town in the world. As you read, notice all the details that describe the town. What are some things you can see, hear, and do there? What town is the best town in the world to you?*

All my life I've heard about
a little, dirt-road,
one-store,
country town
not far from a rocky canyon
way back
in the Texas hills.

This town had lots of space
around it
with caves to find
and honey trees
and giant rocks to climb.

It had a creek
and there were panther tracks

to follow
and you could swing
on the wild grapevines.
My father said it was
the best town in the world
and he just happened
to be born there.
How's that for being
lucky?

We always liked
to hear about
that town
where everything was
perfect.

Of course it had a name
but people called the town
and all the ranches

and the farms around it
just *The Canyon,*
and they called each other
*Canyon People.*
The way my father said it,
you could tell
it was a special thing
to be
one of those people.

All the best cooks
in the world lived there.
My father said
if you were walking down
    the road,
just hunting **arrowheads**
or maybe coming home
    from school,
they'd call you in

**arrowheads:** the
pointed tips of
arrows made by
Native Americans
long ago

and give you
sweet potato pie
or gingerbread
and stand there
by the big wood stove
and smile at you
while you were eating.

It was that kind
of town.
The best blackberries
in the world
grew wild.

My father says
the ones in stores
don't taste a thing
like those
he used to pick.

*Those* tasted just like
a blackberry should.

He'd crawl into
a tangle
of blackberry **thicket**
and eat all he wanted
and finally
walk home
swinging his bucket
(with enough for four pies)
and his hands
and his face
and his hard bare feet
would be stained
that beautiful color.

All plants
liked

**thicket:** bushes

to grow there.
The town was famous for
red **chiles**
and for melons
and for sweet corn, too.

And it's a well-known fact
that chickens in that canyon
laid prettier brown eggs
than chickens
twenty miles on down the road.

My father says
no scientist
has figured out
why.

The dogs were smarter there.
They helped you herd the goats
and growled at rattlesnakes
before you even saw them.
And if you stopped
to climb a tree
your dogs stopped, too.
They curled up and waited
for you to come down.
They didn't run off
by themselves.

Summer days
were longer there
than they are
in other places,
and wildflowers grew taller
and thicker on the hills—
not just the yellow ones.
There were all shades of
lavender and purple
and orange and red
and blue
and the palest kind of pink.
They all had butterflies
to match.

Fireflies lit up
the whole place
at night,
and in the distance
you could hear
somebody's fiddle
or banjo
or harp.

My father says
no city water
ever tasted half as good
as water that he carried

**chiles:** red pepper plants used to make a hot spice

in a bucket from the well
by their back door.

And there isn't
any water
anywhere
as clear
as the water
in that ice cold creek
where all the children
swam.
You could look down
and see the white sand
and watch the minnows
flashing by.

But
when my father came
to the part
about that ice cold water
we would always say,
"It doesn't sound
so perfect
if the water was
*ice cold.*"

He'd look surprised
and say,
"But that's the way
creek water
is supposed to be—
ice cold."

So we learned that
however
things were
in that town
is just exactly how
things *ought* to be. . . .

People there
did things
in their own way.
For instance—
*spelling.*

Sometimes I'd be
surprised
at how my father
spelled a word
that I'd already learned
at school,
but if I mentioned it,
he'd say,
"The way I spell it
is the way
they spelled it
*there,*
so it must be right."

But my mother said
since we weren't living
*there,*
maybe we should just
go ahead

and spell the way
they do in other places.
So we did,
though we always liked
his way.
Maybe that's part of the reason

it was the best town
in the world.
You could do things
whatever way
seemed good
to you.

*The "best town in the world" also had the best celebrations, the best chocolate cake, the best toys, and the smartest people. What else do you think you'd find in the best town?*

Source: Byrd Baylor, *The Best Town in the World*. New York: Scribner's, 1982.

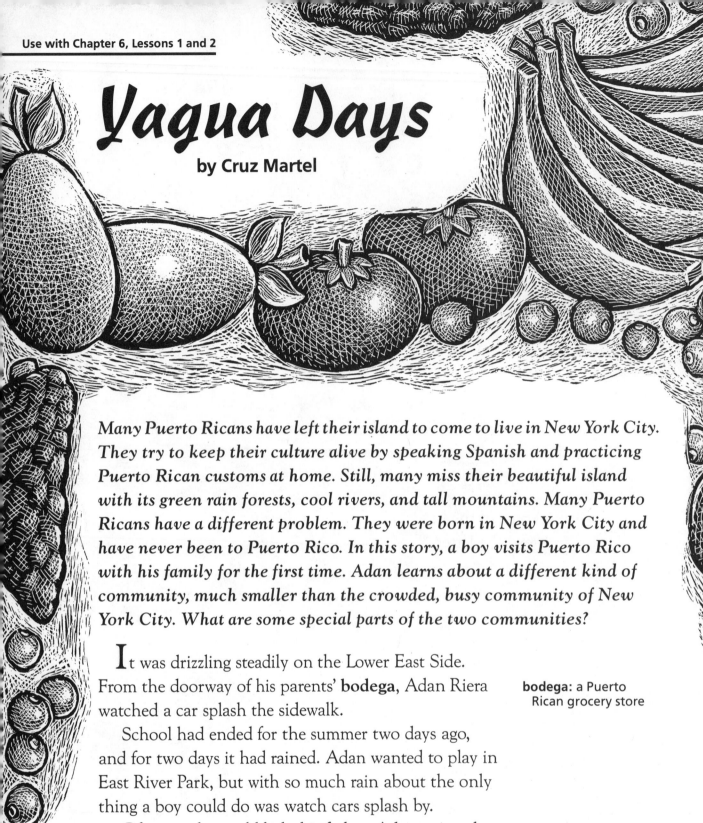

# Yagua Days

## by Cruz Martel

*Many Puerto Ricans have left their island to come to live in New York City. They try to keep their culture alive by speaking Spanish and practicing Puerto Rican customs at home. Still, many miss their beautiful island with its green rain forests, cool rivers, and tall mountains. Many Puerto Ricans have a different problem. They were born in New York City and have never been to Puerto Rico. In this story, a boy visits Puerto Rico with his family for the first time. Adan learns about a different kind of community, much smaller than the crowded, busy community of New York City. What are some special parts of the two communities?*

It was drizzling steadily on the Lower East Side. From the doorway of his parents' **bodega**, Adan Riera watched a car splash the sidewalk.

**bodega:** a Puerto Rican grocery store

School had ended for the summer two days ago, and for two days it had rained. Adan wanted to play in East River Park, but with so much rain about the only thing a boy could do was watch cars splash by.

Of course he could help his father. Adan enjoyed working in the bodega. He liked the smells of the fruits and the different colors of the vegetables, and he liked the way the **mangós, ñames,** and **quenepas** felt in his hands.

But today he would rather be in the park. He watched another car spray past. The rain began to fall harder.

**mangós:** sweet, tropical fruits

**ñames:** tropical vegetables similar to potatoes

**quenepas:** grape-sized fruits with a hard, green peel

Mailman Jorge sloshed in, slapping water off his hat. He smiled. "**Qué pasa**, Adan? Why the long face?"

"Rainy days are terrible days."

"No—they're wonderful days. They're **yagua** days!"

"Stop teasing, Jorge. Yesterday you told me the vegetables and fruits in the bodega are grown in panel trucks. What's a yagua day?"

"**Muchacho**, *this* day is a yagua day. And Puerto Rican vegetables and fruits are grown in trucks. Why, I have a truck myself. Every day I water it!"

Adan's mother and father came in from the back.

"**Hola** Jorge. You look wet."

"I *feel* wetter. But it's a wonderful feeling. It's a yagua-day feeling!"

His mother and father liked Jorge. They had all grown up together in Puerto Rico.

"So you've been telling Adan about yagua days?"

"**Sí. Mira!** Here's a letter for you from **Corral Viejo**, where we all had some of the best yagua days."

Adan's father read the letter. "Good news! My brother Ulise wants Mami, Adan, and me to visit him on his **finca** for two weeks."

"You haven't been to Puerto Rico in years," said Mailman Jorge.

"Adan's *never* been there," replied his mother. "We can ask my brother to take care of the bodega. Adan will meet his family in the mountains at last."

Adan clapped his hands. "Puerto Rico! Who cares about the rain!"

Mailman Jorge smiled. "Maybe you'll even have a few yagua days. **Hasta luego. Y que gocen mucho!**"

**Tío** Ulise met them at the airport in **Ponce**.

"Welcome to Puerto Rico, Adan."

Stocky Uncle Ulise had tiny blue eyes in a round, red face, and big, strong arms, but Adan, excited after his first plane ride, hugged Uncle Ulise even harder than Uncle Ulise hugged him.

**Qué pasa?:** What's happening?

**yagua:** the outer covering of a palm leaf

**muchacho:** boy

**hola:** hello

**Sí. Mira:** Yes, look!
**Corral Viejo:** old corral

**finca:** plántation; farm

**hasta luego:** until we meet again; good-bye

**Y que gocen mucho:** And have fun!

**tío:** uncle

**Ponce:** a seaport in Puerto Rico

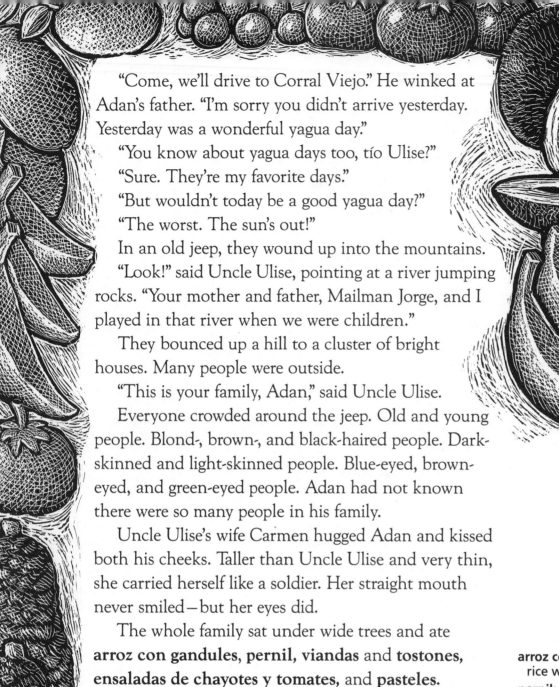

"Come, we'll drive to Corral Viejo." He winked at Adan's father. "I'm sorry you didn't arrive yesterday. Yesterday was a wonderful yagua day."

"You know about yagua days too, tío Ulise?"

"Sure. They're my favorite days."

"But wouldn't today be a good yagua day?"

"The worst. The sun's out!"

In an old jeep, they wound up into the mountains.

"Look!" said Uncle Ulise, pointing at a river jumping rocks. "Your mother and father, Mailman Jorge, and I played in that river when we were children."

They bounced up a hill to a cluster of bright houses. Many people were outside.

"This is your family, Adan," said Uncle Ulise.

Everyone crowded around the jeep. Old and young people. Blond-, brown-, and black-haired people. Dark-skinned and light-skinned people. Blue-eyed, brown-eyed, and green-eyed people. Adan had not known there were so many people in his family.

Uncle Ulise's wife Carmen hugged Adan and kissed both his cheeks. Taller than Uncle Ulise and very thin, she carried herself like a soldier. Her straight mouth never smiled—but her eyes did.

The whole family sat under wide trees and ate **arroz con gandules, pernil, viandas** and **tostones, ensaladas de chayotes y tomates,** and **pasteles.**

Adan talked and sang until his voice turned to a squeak. He ate until his stomach almost popped a pants button.

Afterward he fell asleep under a big mosquito net before the sun had even gone down behind the mountains.

In the morning Uncle Ulise called out, "Adan, everyone ate all the food in the house. Let's get more."

"From a bodega?"

"No, **mi amor.** From my finca on the mountain."

"You drive a tractor and plow on the mountain?"

**arroz con gandules:** rice with pigeon peas

**pernil:** roast pork

**viandas:** Puerto Rican vegetables

**tostones:** fried green plantains; tropical fruits similar to bananas

**ensaladas de chayotes y tomates:** salads of avocados and tomatoes

**pasteles:** Puerto Rican dumplings

**mi amor:** my love

**Tía** Carmen smiled with her eyes. "We don't need tractors and plows on our finca."

"I don't understand."

"**Vente.** You will."

Adan and his parents, Aunt Carmen, and Uncle Ulise hiked up the mountain beside a splashy stream.

Near the top they walked through groves of fruit trees.

"Long ago your grandfather planted these trees," Adan's mother said. "Now Aunt Carmen and Uncle Ulise pick what they need for themselves or want to give away or sell in Ponce."

"Let's work!" said Aunt Carmen.

Sitting on his father's shoulders, Adan picked oranges. Swinging a hooked stick, he pulled down mangós.

Whipping a bamboo pole with a knife tied to the end, he chopped **mapenes** from a tall tree.

Digging with a **machete**, he uncovered ñames.

Finally, gripping a very long pole, he struck down coconuts.

"How do we get all the food down the mountain?" he asked.

"Watch," said Aunt Carmen. She whistled loudly.

Adan saw a patch of white moving in the trees. A horse with a golden mane appeared.

Uncle Ulise fed him a **guanábana**. The horse twitched his ears and munched the delicious fruit loudly.

"Palomo will help us carry all the fruit and vegetables we've picked," Adan's mother said.

Back at the house, Adan gave Palomo another guanábana.

"He'll go back up to the finca now," his father said. "He's got all he wants to eat there."

Uncle Ulise rubbed his knee.

"**Qué te pasa?**" asked Adan's mother.

"My knee. It always hurts just before rain comes."

**tía:** aunt

**vente:** come on

**mapenes:** breadfruits; round fruits that have a texture like that of bread when baked

**machete:** a broad, heavy knife

**guanábana:** a sweet fruit covered with prickly skin

**Qué te pasa?:** what's the matter?

Adan looked at the cloudless sky. "But it's not going to rain."

"Yes, it will. My knee never lies. It'll rain tonight. Maybe tomorrow. Say! When it does, it'll be a yagua day!"

In the morning Adan, waking up cozy under his mosquito net, heard rain banging on the metal roof and **coquies** beeping like tiny car horns.

**coquies:** tree frogs

He jumped out of bed and got a big surprise. His mother and father, Uncle Ulise, and Aunt Carmen were on the porch wearing bathing suits.

"**Vamonos**, Adan," his father said. "It's a wonderful yagua day. Put on your bathing suit!"

**Vamonos:** let's go

In the forest he heard shouts and swishing noises in the rain.

Racing into a clearing, he saw boys and girls shooting down a runway of grass, then disappearing over a rock ledge.

Uncle Ulise picked up a canoelike object from the grass. "This is a yagua, Adan. It fell from this palm tree."

"And this is what we do with it," said his father. He ran, then belly-flopped on the yagua. He skimmed down the grass, sailed up into the air, and vanished over the ledge. His mother found another yagua and did the same.

"Papi! Mami!"

Uncle Ulise laughed. "Don't worry, Adan. They won't hurt themselves. The river is down there. It pools beneath the ledge. The rain turns the grass butter-slick so you can zip into the water. That's what makes it a yagua day! Come and join us!"

That day Adan found out what fun a yagua day is!

*Adan returned to New York, full of stories to tell about yagua days in Puerto Rico. What did Adan learn about Puerto Rico? Do you think he will miss the island? What do you think he learned by visiting a different community?*

Source: Cruz Martel, *Yagua Days*. New York: Dial, 1976.

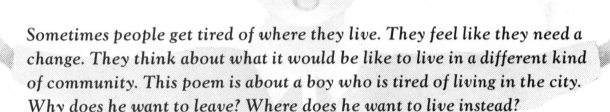

# Rudolph Is Tired of the City

## by Gwendolyn Brooks

*Sometimes people get tired of where they live. They feel like they need a change. They think about what it would be like to live in a different kind of community. This poem is about a boy who is tired of living in the city. Why does he want to leave? Where does he want to live instead?*

These buildings are too close to me.

I'd like to PUSH away.

I'd like to live in the country,

And spread my arms all day.

I'd like to spread my breath out, too—

As farmers' sons and daughters do.

I'd tend the cows and chickens.

I'd do the other chores.

Then, all the hours left I'd go

A-SPREADING out-of-doors.

*Do you ever get tired of where you live? What makes you want to live someplace else? What type of community would you rather live in? What do you think you would like better about it?*

Source: Gwendolyn Brooks,
*Bronzeville Boys and Girls*. New York: Harper, 1956.

# Rhyme-Time Fun

## Traditional Rhymes

*Rhymes are a traditional part of many popular American games. There are jump rope rhymes and rhymes for hand-clapping and ball-bouncing games. Here are some favorite rhymes that have been recited, chanted, and sung as part of games for many years. Which ones do you already know? Which ones are new to you?*

## JUMP-ROPE RHYMES

*Jumping rope is popular just about everywhere. Here are a few of the rhymes and chants children in the United States have been jumping to for years.*

### Engine, Engine

*In this rhyme, you keep repeating the last line until the jumper misses. If the jumper misses on "no," that means no money back!*

Engine, engine, number nine,
Running on Chicago line.
If the train should jump the track,
Will I get my money back?
Yes, no, maybe so. . .

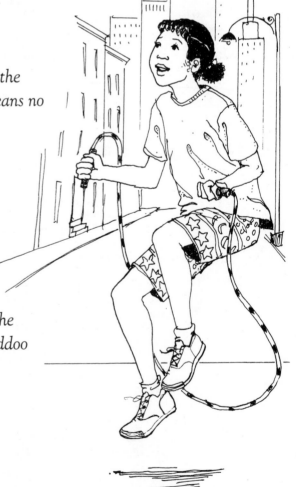

### Teddy Bear, Teddy Bear

*This one is tricky. You have to turn around, touch the ground, show your shoe (kick out one foot), and skiddoo (run out), while the rope is turning!*

Teddy bear, teddy bear, turn around,
Teddy bear, teddy bear, touch the ground.
Teddy bear, teddy bear, show your shoe,
Teddy bear, teddy bear, now skiddoo!

# HAND-CLAPPING RHYMES

*Do you like to play clapping games with a friend? Here is one clapping rhyme you may already know. Make up your own clapping pattern for the last rhyme. Try crossing hands, slapping thighs, snapping fingers, patting heads—anything! See how fast you and your partner can go!*

## Miss Mary Mack

Miss Mary Mack, Mack, Mack,
All dressed in black, black, black,
With silver buttons, buttons, buttons,
All down her back, back, back.
She asked her mother, mother, mother,
For fifty cents, cents, cents,

To see the cows, cows, cows,
Jump over the fence, fence, fence.
They jumped so high, high, high,
They reached the sky, sky, sky,
And never came back, back, back,
Till the fourth of July, -ly, -ly!

| | |
|---|---|
| Miss | *Cross hands and clap your shoulders.* |
| Mar- | *Uncross arms and clap your thighs.* |
| -y | *Clap your own hands together.* |
| Mack | *Clap right hands with your partner.* |
| —(pause) | *Clap your own hands together.* |
| Mack | *Clap left hands with your partner.* |
| —(pause) | *Clap your own hands together.* |
| Mack | *Clap both hands with your partner.* |
| | (Continue the same pattern.) |

# STREET RHYMES

## Say There, Fellow

*One person or the entire group does the dance steps suggested.*

Say there, Fellow, you can't talk;
I'll turn my back and do the camelwalk!

Say there, Fellow, you can't whistle;
I'll turn my back and do the bicycle!

Say there, Fellow, you can't crack!
I'll turn my back and do the applejack!

## Ooo-ah, Wanna Piece of Pie

Ooo-ah, wanna piece of pie,
Pie too sweet, wanna piece of meat,
Meat too tough, wanna ride a bus,
Bus too full, wanna ride a bull,
Bull too fat, want your money back,
Money too green, wanna jelly bean,
Jelly bean not cooked, wanna read a book,
Book not read, wanna go to bed.
So close your eyes and count to ten,
And if you miss, start all over again.

## BALL-BOUNCING RHYMES

### A, My Name is Alice

*This alphabet game is probably the most popular ball-bouncing game of all. Bounce the ball on every other word in the rhyme and lift your leg over the ball on each alphabet word. Make up verses for each letter of the alphabet as long as you can keep bouncing the ball and thinking of names, places, and things to sell.*

A, my name is Alice,
And my husband's name is Al.
We come from Alabama,
And we sell apples.
B, my name is Betty,
And my husband's name is Bob.
We come from Boston,
And we sell beans.

C, my name is Clara,
And my husband's name is Carl.
We come from Chicago,
And we sell cats.
D, my name is Donna,
And my husband's name is Dave.
We come from Denver,
And we sell doughnuts.

*These rhymes are American traditions. They have been handed down from generation to generation. What rhymes do you know? Where did you learn them? Will you pass them on to others?*

Sources: Margaret Taylor Burroughs, *Did You Feed My Cow?* Chicago: Follett Publishing Company, 1969; Joanna Cole and Stephanie Calmenson, *Miss Mary Mack*. New York: Morrow Junior Books, 1990; Carl Withers, *A Rocket in My Pocket*. New York: Holt, Rinehart and Winston, 1948.

# Picking Berries

### by Aileen Fisher

*Long ago, people lived off the land, picking wild plants and hunting wild animals. Berries were one of their main foods. Today, many kinds of berries are grown on fruit farms and others still grow wild in rural areas. In the poem below, Aileen Fisher describes a day spent picking berries. How does the poem make you feel you were there?*

All day long
we picked and picked.

The sun was strong,
the bushes pricked.

The berries grew
in **brambly** places          **brambly:** full of thorns
where twigs untied
my sneaker laces.

We picked and picked
and picked some more.
The sun blazed down,
my arms got sore,

And then all night
as time went ticking
I dreamed I still
kept picking, picking.

*Picking berries by hand can be lots of fun. But picking berries day after day, as many farm workers do, is very hard work. Have you ever picked berries? What's your favorite kind?*

Source: Lee Bennett Hopkins, ed., *On the Farm*. Boston: Little, Brown, 1991.

# How PIZZA Came to Queens

## by Dayal Kaur Khalsa

*One of the most important things produced on a dairy farm is milk. People use milk to make butter, ice cream, and hot chocolate. They also use milk to make cheese—which is used to make pizza! Before 1950 few people in the United States ate pizza. Do you know where pizza came from in the first place? In the following selection from Dayal Kaur Khalsa's story, we find out how pizza came to the Queens area of New York City. Linda, Judy, and Peggy Penny are surprised to learn that Mrs. Pelligrino, a distant cousin from Italy, is coming to visit. Mrs. Pelligrino enjoys her visit, but she misses something the girls have never heard of, "pizza." The three sisters, together with their best friend May, decide to find out what pizza is so they can make Mrs. Pelligrino happy. Do you think this could really be the way pizza came to Queens?*

The girls had grown very fond of Mrs. Pelligrino. They wanted to make her really happy at least once before she had to leave. The key seemed to be connected to the word *pizza*. If only they could find out what it meant. May had an idea where they could try.

They went to the library. The librarian helped them look it up in the dictionary: *piz-za* (pēt′ sə) n: an Italian baked dish consisting of a shallow pie-like crust covered usually with a spiced mixture of tomatoes and cheese.

"Pie-like? With tomatoes?" said Peggy.

Judy suggested they look in a cookbook.

They had to look in a lot of cookbooks before they finally found one with a recipe for *Pizza Pie*. Peggy

copied out the list of ingredients: yeast, flour, tomato paste, mozzarella cheese, parmesan cheese, olive oil, garlic, oregano, and pepper.

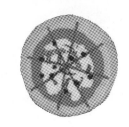

"It sure doesn't sound like pie to me," said May.

"Yuk," said Linda. They all agreed it sounded terrible. But—if it would make Mrs. Pelligrino happy—they would try anything.

The next day they went shopping and bought everything on the list.

Mrs. Pelligrino knocked on the wall of their play store. "What you got for me today?" she asked.

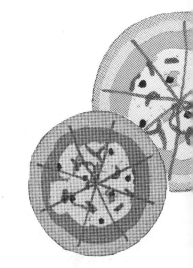

May and Linda began handing her the things they had bought. With each item her smile grew bigger. By the time they gave her the garlic Mrs. Pelligrino was beaming. "Pizza!" she cried joyfully. She cradled the ingredients in her arms and hurried into the house. She looked very, very happy.

Mrs. Pelligrino brought her strangely shaped green package down to the kitchen and put it on the table. May and Linda still hoped it might be a present. She unwrapped it carefully. It was—a rolling pin! Mrs. Pelligrino smiled at it like an old friend. May and Linda frowned. "No be sad," said Mrs. Pelligrino. "We make pizza."

She showed them how to make dough and then roll it out into a circle with the rolling pin. Then she taught them how to throw the dough high in the air to stretch it. She spread tomato sauce on each big circle and the girls sprinkled them with cheese.

As the pizza baked and the cheese began to bubble,

the whole house was filled with the most wonderful smell they had ever smelled. It smelled as good as toast and french fries and ketchup and grilled cheese sandwiches and spaghetti all rolled into one. They sniffed in long and deep.

Mrs. Penny came into the kitchen. "What is that delicious smell?" she asked.

"It's pizza!" they cried.

When the pizza was done, they had a party. May called her grandma to come over, and the mailman, who happened to be delivering the mail just then, joined in. Everyone thought pizza was the best thing they ever tasted.

Mrs. Pelligrino was very happy. "Ah, pizza! Is good, no?" she said proudly.

"Yes!" they all yelled.

And that's how pizza came to Queens.

*Mrs. Pelligrino is not a real person. But Queens is a real place that has many pizzerias, and pizza really does come from Italy. In fact, pizza is the Italian word for "pie." Many foods Americans eat come from countries outside the United States. Did you know that hamburgers and frankfurters come from Germany? And that sandwiches were first made in England? Of course, egg rolls are a Chinese food, and tacos come from Mexico. What are your favorite foods? Do you know where they come from?*

Source: Dayal Kaur Khalsa, *How Pizza Came to Queens*. New York: Potter, 1989.

# The Patchwork Quilt

## by Valerie Flournoy

*Neighborhood picnics and festivals are traditions you have read about. Quilting is a rural tradition that began when people did not have enough money for cloth. People saved scraps of fabric from old clothing and stitched them together to make quilts. In this story, Tanya's grandmother carries on the tradition by making a patchwork quilt using scraps from the family's old clothing. How does the quilt bring the family together?*

Grandma held Tanya close and patted her head. "It's gonna take quite a while to make this quilt, not a couple of days or a week—not even a month. A good quilt, a **masterpiece**..." Grandma's eyes shone at the thought. "Why I need more material. More gold and blue, some red and green. And I'll need the time to do it right. It'll take me a year at least."

**masterpiece:** a great work of art

"A year," shouted Tanya. "That's too long. I can't wait that long, Grandma."

Grandma laughed. "A year ain't that long, honey. Makin' this quilt gonna be a joy. Now run along and let Grandma rest." Grandma turned her head toward the sunlight and closed her eyes.

"I'm gonna make a masterpiece," she murmured, clutching a scrap of cloth in her hand, just before she fell asleep.

"We'll have to get you a new pair and use these old ones for rags," Mama said as she hung the last piece of wash on the clothesline one August afternoon.

Jim was miserable. His favorite blue corduroy pants had been held together with patches; now they were beyond repair.

"Bring them here," Grandma said.

Grandma took part of the pant leg and cut a few blue squares. Jim gave her a hug and watched her add his patches to the others.

"A quilt won't forget. It can tell your life story," she said.

The arrival of autumn meant school and Halloween. This year Tanya would be an African princess. She danced around in the long, flowing robes Mama had made from several yards of colorful material. The old bracelets and earrings Tanya had found in a trunk in the attic jingled noisily as she moved. Grandma cut some squares out of the leftover scraps and added Tanya to the quilt too!

The days grew colder but Tanya and her brothers didn't mind. They knew snow wasn't far away. Mama **dreaded** winter's coming. Every year she would **plead with** Grandma to move away from the **drafty** window, but Grandma wouldn't **budge**.

**dreaded:** feared
**plead with:** beg
**drafty:** where air comes in
**budge:** move a bit

"Grandma, please," Mama scolded. "You can sit here by the heater."

"I'm not your grandmother, I'm your mother," Grandma said. "And I'm gonna sit here in **the Lord's light** and make my masterpiece."

**the Lord's light:** sunlight

It was the end of November when Ted, Jim, and Tanya got their wish. They awoke one morning to find everything in sight covered with snow. Tanya got dressed and flew down the stairs. Ted and Jim, and even Mama and Papa, were already outside.

"I don't like leaving Grandma in that house by herself," Mama said. "I know she's lonely."

Tanya pulled herself out of the snow, being careful not to ruin her angel. "Grandma isn't lonely," Tanya said happily. "She and the quilt are telling each other stories."

Mama glanced questioningly at Tanya, "Telling each other stories?"

"Yes, Grandma says a quilt never forgets!"

The family spent the morning and most of the afternoon sledding down the hill. Finally, when they were all **numb** from the cold, they went inside for hot chocolate and sandwiches.

"I think I'll go sit and talk to Grandma," Mama said.

"Then she can explain to you about our quilt—our very own family quilt," Tanya said.

Mama saw the **mischievous glint** in her youngest child's eyes.

"Why, I may just have her do that, young lady," Mama said as she walked out of the kitchen.

Tanya leaned over the table to see into the living room. Grandma was **hunched** over, her eyes close to the fabric as she made tiny stitches. Mama sat at the old woman's feet. Tanya couldn't hear what was said but she knew Grandma was telling Mama all about quilts and how this quilt would be very special. Tanya sipped her chocolate slowly, then she saw Mama pick up a piece of fabric, rub it with her fingers, and smile.

From that moment on both women spent their winter evenings working on the quilt. Mama did the sewing while Grandma cut the fabrics and placed the scraps in a pattern of colors. Even while they were cooking and baking all their Christmas specialties during the day, at night they still worked on the quilt. Only once did Mama put it aside. She wanted to wear something special Christmas night, so she bought some gold material and made a beautiful dress. Tanya knew without asking that the gold scraps would be in the quilt too.

There was much singing and laughing that Christmas. All Grandma's sons and daughters and nieces and nephews came to **pay their respects**. The Christmas tree lights shone brightly, filling the room with sparkling colors. Later, when everyone had gone home, Papa said he had never felt so much happiness in the house. And Mama agreed.

When Tanya got downstairs the next morning, she found Papa fixing pancakes.

**numb:** unable to feel or move

**mischievous:** playful, naughty
**glint:** sparkle

**hunched:** bent

"Is today a special day, too?" asked Jim.

"Where's Mama?" asked Tanya.

"Grandma doesn't feel well this morning," Papa said. "Your mother is with her now till the doctor gets here."

"Will Grandma be all right?" Ted asked.

Papa rubbed his son's head and smiled. "There's nothing for you to worry about. We'll take care of Grandma."

Tanya looked into the living room. There on the back of the big chair rested the patchwork quilt. It was folded neatly, just as Grandma had left it.

"Mother didn't want us to know she wasn't feeling well. She thought it would spoil our Christmas," Mama told them later, her face **drawn** and tired, her eyes a puffy red. "Now it's up to all of us to be quiet and make her as comfortable as possible." Papa put an arm around Mama's shoulder.

**drawn: worn out, thin**

"Can we see Grandma?" Tanya asked.

"No, not tonight," Papa said. "Grandma needs plenty of rest."

It was nearly a week, the day before New Year's, before the children were **permitted** to see their grandmother. She looked tired and spoke in whispers.

**permitted: allowed**

"We miss you, Grandma," Ted said.

"And your muffins and hot chocolate," added Jim. Grandma smiled.

"Your quilt misses you too, Grandma," Tanya said. Grandma's smile faded from her lips. Her eyes grew cloudy.

"My masterpiece," Grandma sighed. "It would have been beautiful. Almost half finished." The old woman closed her eyes and turned away from her grandchildren. Papa whispered it was time to leave. Ted, Jim, and Tanya crept from the room.

Tanya walked slowly to where the quilt lay. She had seen Grandma and Mama work on it. Tanya thought real hard. She knew how to cut the scraps, but she wasn't certain of the rest. Just then Tanya felt a hand resting on her shoulder. She looked up and saw Mama.

"Tomorrow," Mama said.

New Year's Day was the beginning. After the dishes were washed and put away, Tanya and Mama examined the quilt.

"You cut more squares, Tanya, while I stitch some patches together," Mama said.

Tanya snipped and trimmed the scraps of material till her hands hurt from the scissors. Mama watched her carefully, making sure the squares were all the same size. The next day was the same as the last. More snipping and cutting. But Mama couldn't always be around to watch Tanya work. Grandma had to be looked after. So Tanya worked by herself. Then one night, as Papa read them stories, Jim walked over and looked at the quilt. In it he saw patches of blue. His blue. Without saying a word Jim picked up the scissors and some scraps and started to make squares. Ted helped Jim put the squares in piles while Mama showed Tanya how to join them.

Every day, as soon as she got home from school, Tanya worked on the quilt. Ted and Jim were too busy with sports, and Mama was looking after Grandma, so Tanya worked alone. But after a few weeks she stopped. Something was wrong—something was missing, Tanya thought. For days the quilt lay on the back of the chair. No one knew why Tanya had stopped working. Tanya would sit and look at the quilt. Finally she knew. Something wasn't missing. Someone was missing from the quilt.

That evening before she went to bed Tanya tiptoed into Grandma's room, a pair of scissors in her hand. She quietly lifted the end of Grandma's old quilt and carefully removed a few squares.

February and March came and went as Mama proudly watched her daughter work on the last few rows of patches. Tanya always found time for the quilt. Grandma had been watching too. The old woman had been getting stronger and stronger as the months passed. Once she was able, Papa would carry Grandma to her chair by the window. "I need the Lord's light," Grandma said. Then she would sit and hum softly to herself and watch Tanya work.

"Yes, honey, this quilt is nothin' but a joy," Grandma said.

Summer vacation was almost here. One June day Tanya came home to find Grandma working on the quilt again! She had finished sewing the last few squares together; the stuffing was in place, and she was already pinning on the backing.

"Grandma!" Tanya shouted.

Grandma looked up. "Hush, child. It's almost time to do the quilting on these patches. But first I have some special finishing touches...."

The next night Grandma cut the final thread with her teeth. "There. It's done," she said. Mama helped Grandma spread the quilt full length.

Nobody had realized how big it had gotten or how beautiful. Reds, greens, blues, and golds, light shades and dark, blended in and out throughout the quilt.

"It's beautiful," Papa said. He touched the gold patch, looked at Mama, and remembered. Jim remembered too. There was his blue and the red from Ted's shirt. There was Tanya's Halloween costume. And there was Grandma. Even though her patch was old, it fit right in.

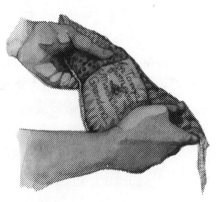

They all remembered the past year. They especially remembered Tanya and all her work. So it had been decided. In the right hand corner of the last row of patches was delicately stitched, "For Tanya from your Mama and Grandma."

*What did Grandma mean when she said "A quilt won't forget"? Suppose you were to make a family quilt. What are some patches from old clothing or other material you would use? What memories would they help you keep?*

Source: Valerie Flournoy, *The Patchwork Quilt*. New York: Dial, 1985.

# Sing a Song of People

### by Lois Lenski

*Cities are busy places. They are full of lots and lots of people. Sometimes it's fun to watch all the people coming and going in a busy city. In the following poem, Lois Lenski describes the many different people she sees in the city. Read the poem once. Then read it again aloud. How is the poem like a song?*

Sing a song of people
  Walking fast or slow;
People in the city,
  Up and down they go.
  People on the sidewalk,
  People on the bus;
  People passing, passing,
  In back and front of us.
People on the subway
Underneath the ground;
People riding in taxis
Round and round and round.
People with their hats on,
  Going in the doors;
People with umbrellas
  When it rains and pours.

People in tall buildings
And in stores below;
Riding elevators
Up and down they go.
People walking singly,
People in a crowd;
People saying nothing,
People talking loud.
People laughing, smiling,
Grumpy people too;
People who just hurry
And never look at you!
Sing a song of people
  Who like to come and go;
Sing of city people
  You see but never know!

*There sure were a lot of people in that poem! Did the poem sound busy and fast? Did it hurry along just like the people in the city? Could you hear the sing-song rhythm? Work with a small group. Make up a tune for the poem and try singing it for the rest of your class. Have fun!*

Source: Jack Prelutsky, ed., *The Random House Book of Poetry for Children*. New York: Random House, 1983.

# IN A NEIGHBORHOOD IN LOS ANGELES

## by Francisco X. Alarcón

*Many Mexicans have come to live in the United States. The poet Francisco X. Alarcón is a Mexican American who was born in Los Angeles. In this poem he remembers his grandmother who took care of him when he was young. What did he learn from her?*

| En un Barrio de Los Angeles | In a Neighborhood in Los Angeles |
|---|---|
| el español | I learned |
| lo aprendí | Spanish |
| de mi abuela | from my grandma |
| | |
| mijito | **mijito** |
| no llores | don't cry |
| me decía | she'd tell me |
| | |
| en las mañanas | on the mornings |
| cuando salían | my parents |
| mis padres | would leave |
| | |
| a trabajar | to work |
| en las canerías | at the fish |
| de pescado | **canneries** |
| | |
| mi abuela | my grandma |
| platicaba | would chat |
| con las sillas | with chairs |
| | |
| les cantaba | sing them |
| canciones | old |
| antiguas | songs |
| | |
| les bailaba | dance |
| valses en | waltzes with them |
| la cocina | in the kitchen |
| | |
| cuando decía | when she'd say |
| niño barrigón | **niño barrigón** |
| se reía | she'd laugh |

mijito: my grandson

canneries: factories where food is put into cans

niño barrigón: chubby little boy

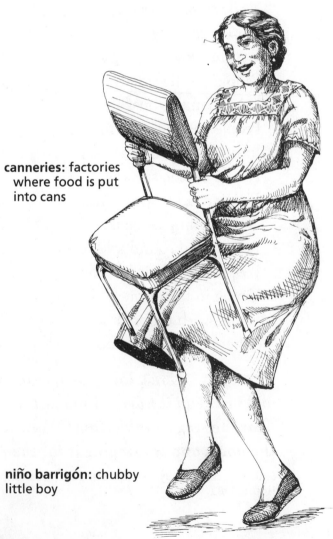

|  |  |
|---|---|
| con mi abuela | with my grandma |
| aprendí | I learned |
| a contar nubes | to count clouds |
| | |
| a reconocer | to point out |
| en las macetas | in flowerpots |
| la yerbabuena | mint leaves |
| | |
| mi abuela | my grandma |
| llevaba lunas | wore moons |
| en el vestido | on her dress |
| | |
| la montaña | Mexico's mountains |
| el desierto | deserts |
| el mar de México | ocean |
| | |
| en sus ojos | in her eyes |
| yo los veía | I'd see them |
| en sus trenzas | in her braids |
| | |
| yo los tocaba | I'd touch them |
| con su voz | in her voice |
| yo los olia | smell them |
| | |
| un día | one day |
| me dijeron | I was told: |
| se fue muy lejos | she went far away |
| | |
| pero yo aún | but still |
| las siento | I feel her |
| conmigo | with me |
| | |
| diciéndome | whispering |
| quedito al oído | in my ear |
| mijito | *mijito* |

*The poet's grandmother taught him things about Mexican culture. She taught him Spanish, old songs and dances, and she reminded him of Mexico. What have you learned from people in your family? Have they taught you about your culture?*

Source: Francisco X. Alarcón, *Body in Flames/Cuerpo en Llamas.* San Francisco, CA: Chronicle Books, 1990.

# The City Blues

## American Folk Blues

*Have you ever heard people say they had the blues? They meant they were feeling sad or lonely. The blues is also a kind of music first sung by African Americans. Many blues songs tell about sad and hard times. Other blues songs are not sad at all. Here is a blues song about visiting cities like Seattle for the first time. How do you think the traveler feels?*

1. Cloud - y in the west, Looks like rain;— I spent all my mon - ey on the sub - way train— in New York Ci - ty,— In New York Ci - ty,— In New York Ci - ty, you real - ly got to know your way.—

2. Went to Detroit, it was fine,
   I watched the cars movin' off
     th' assembly line,
   In Detroit City, In Detroit City,
   In Detroit City, you really got
     to know your way.

3. I looped the loop, I rocked and reeled,
   I thought the Cubs played ball
     in Marshall Field,
   In the Windy City, in the Windy City,
   In the Windy City, you really got
     to know your way.

4. Went a little south, St. Louis (Loo-ee),
   A piece of Missouri on the Mississippi,
   In old St. Louis, in old St. Louis,
   In old St. Louis, you really got
     to know your way.

5. I moved on down, New Orleans (Or-leens).
   I had my first taste of its pecan pralines,
   In New Orleans, in New Orleans,
   In New Orleans, you really got
     to know your way.

6. I headed West, to "L.A."
   It really is a city where it's fun to stay,
   In old "L.A.," in old "L.A.,"
   In old "L.A.." you really got
     to know your way.

7. Headed up the coast, "Golden Gate."
   I went out to the wharf to eat a
     "Fisherman's Plate,"
   In San Francisco, in San Francisco,
   In San Francisco, you really got
     to know your way.

# Working on an Assembly Line by Chuck Hilt

*Working on an assembly line is a hard job. It demands skill, quick thinking, and teamwork. Chuck Hilt knows this as well as anyone. He works in a large factory that builds pickup trucks. His job is to fill in for any worker who is absent. His job changes from day to day. In the following selection, Chuck Hilt describes what it is like to work on an assembly line. What does he like about his job? Why is it important for him to work with other people?*

In our assembly **plant**, we have five different departments: trim, cab shop, paint, **chassis**, and the final line. Each one of those departments **assembles** a part of the truck. All parts join at the final line to create a truck. And that's basically what our plant does: we assemble parts that are shipped to us. Some things come in **preassembled**, like seats. They're assembled at other places and we get them in **through freight**. Then we bolt them down and create a truck.

We have about 2,500 people working out here. I usually work in the trim area. My team handles all of the glass: the mirrors, the crank-up windows in the doors, and the windshields. We **install** all the parts related to glass, such as the door handles and the inside molding. When the body leaves trim, it goes over and meets up with the chassis department. This department assembles the engine, the wheels, and the frame. Then they drop the body down on the chassis. On the final line they put the front panels around the engine.

**plant:** factory

**chassis [chas'ē]:** frame that supports the body of a car

**asembles:** puts together

**preassembled:** already built

**through freight:** by transportation from other factories

**install:** put in place

81

Some people like knowing what they're going to be doing when they come in to work. They like to know they're going to be on a certain job. But I like coming in and doing different jobs. To me it makes the time go faster.

I take pride in what I do. I like to do a **quality** job. I like to try to do everything right. I get satisfaction out of seeing one of our trucks in a parking lot. I get a kick out of seeing the product that we built. I find myself wondering what job I was doing when that one was built, if I was putting in door pads or windshields or whatever.

As a member of a work team, I've become close with the team members. We joke. That's how I pass a lot of time—keeping a lot of joking going. We pay attention to the job. We don't want to get to where we're joking so much that we let something slide. But cracking a joke now and then, making conversation about something that's going on, talking sports—all that contributes to making time go faster. If I get along well with my team, things seem to go a whole lot better.

This work is basically the same as a sports team. Same idea. Like a football team: you've got a quarterback, linemen, and running backs. When everybody does what they're supposed to do, then the play is successful. That's the same way with building a truck. One person can't build a truck. It takes a whole team. If one person lacks, or **slacks**, or isn't doing his job, or is not able to get something on, I might not be able to put my part on. And me not putting my part on might affect somebody else. That's why it's important for everybody to work together and make sure they do it right the first time.

**quality:** first-rate

**slacks:** slows

*Assembly-line workers like Chuck Hilt play a key role in our country's economy. They build products that people want and need. By providing jobs, factories make communities stronger. People like Chuck Hilt make these factories work to keep our country moving.*

Source: Adapted from Neil Johnson, *All in a Day's Work: Twelve Americans Talk About Their Jobs.* Boston: Little, Brown, and Company, 1989.

# The House on Hillside La

**by Johanna Hurwitz**

*Many families move to the suburbs because there's more room. They can live in a house with a backyard. They can escape the crowds and noise of the city. In this selection, a boy and his family move from New York City to a suburb in New Jersey. What are some of the things that are different there?*

It was bedtime and the light was out.

Aldo Sossi lay in bed trying to fall asleep. The bed was his old one, but the bedroom was new. This morning the Sossi family had moved from New York City to Woodside, New Jersey. There were so many thoughts jumping about in Aldo's head that he couldn't relax and go to sleep. Tomorrow he would start attending the fourth grade at the Woodside School.

"Nobody moves and starts a new school in the middle of the year," Elaine, his older sister, had complained to their parents.

"This is January fifth," Mr. Sossi had answered. "It's not exactly the middle of the year."

But for the Sossi children, Elaine and Karen and Aldo, the year seemed to begin when school opened in

September. Having their father change jobs and make the family move in January seemed very difficult.

Actually, when Mr. Sossi had told his children about the proposed move to New Jersey, it had seemed very exciting. Elaine and Karen, who were fourteen and twelve and a half, were delighted that they were going to have their own private rooms. Their mother promised the children that they could invite their old city friends to come and sleep over when there was a school vacation. And they liked the thought of living in their own house and having a backyard, an upstairs and a downstairs, a fireplace, and an attic.

Aldo remembered the Saturday about a month ago when the family had driven out to visit their new home. It was located on Hillside La, which seemed odd since the area was actually on level ground. The real address was 17 Hillside Lane. *La* was an abbreviation, and all the street signs they passed used the short form: Forest La, Maple La, Cherry La, and finally their own Hillside La.

"**Quelle maison!**" shouted Elaine, when the car stopped. She was studying French this year at school, and she liked to use French words whenever she could. Mrs. Sossi had studied French years ago but had forgotten it all. So no one could be sure what Elaine was saying, and if she sometimes made a mistake, no one could correct her.

**Quelle maison!: What a house!**

Aldo noticed with pleasure that their new house was really several houses. First, there was the house that they would all live in. Then there was a garage, which was the house for the car. In the city they had just parked the car out on the street. There was also a doghouse in the yard, and finally, hanging from an old maple tree, there was a little birdhouse.

"Will we get a dog to live in the doghouse?" Aldo had asked his parents eagerly. Aldo loved animals, and he had wanted a dog for as long as he could remember.

"I don't know. Let's wait and see how things work out," said his mother. "Maybe the cats will want the house for themselves," she said. The Sossi family had two cats, Peabody and Poughkeepsie.

"Will the cats go outdoors?" wondered Karen. In the city the cats were always kept inside the apartment. Life in the suburbs was obviously going to mean a lot of changes for them all, even the cats.

They had gone inside, and each of the Sossi children had picked out a bedroom. It was fun walking through the empty rooms and hearing their voices echoing as they called out their discoveries to one another.

"**Voila!**" Elaine shouted. "This room has a window seat!"

Karen found a closet that was so big it had a window inside it.

Aldo was interested in everything. He went down to the basement, where there was a furnace and a washing machine and a dryer. He **investigated** the attic, which had nothing in it but dust and old spider webs.

Mrs. Sossi was **mentally** moving all their furniture about. "Let's put the sofa here." She pointed to one area of the living room. "And we can put the television over here."

It had been a very exciting day, and Aldo, watching squirrels chase one another up and down the maple tree in the backyard, had tried not to think how nervous he would feel when the time came to start the new school.

**Voila!**: There it is!

**investigated**: searched carefully

**mentally**: in the mind

*Aldo worries about starting a new school and making new friends. Do you think moving is difficult for this reason? What other changes might be hard to get used to? Suppose your family could move to a different kind of community. Would you want to move? Why or why not?*

Source: Johanna Hurwitz, *Aldo Applesauce*. New York: William Morrow, 1979.

# FIELD

### by
### Frank Asch

*Many places have changed from small towns to suburbs like Austell, Georgia. Instead of farm fields, there are houses with lawns. Some people in the suburbs work hard at taking care of their lawns. They plant seeds, spread fertilizer, water the grass with a sprinkler, and mow it every week. They even try to make their lawns greener and neater than their neighbors'. Other people, like Frank Asch who wrote this poem, just wish the lawn was a field again. What does he miss about the way it used to be?*

I see my neighbor
cutting his green lawn
and I remember when it used to
   be just a field.
I remember the weeds
and the wild flowers
changing colors with the seasons,
never looking quite the same.
I remember the crack
of wild asparagus stalks
as I picked them and brought
   them home
for my mother to cook.

I remember the milkweed
   blowing
in the fall wind
and the frosty snow
whistling through the brown
skeletons of Queen Anne's lace.
And I remember springtime
soggy and green
light green dark green moss green
with flecks of red
and even the green
of what it is now,
just a lawn.

*Taking care of a home is a big responsibility. There are lots of things to take care of inside and out. Besides mowing the lawn, what are some jobs that have to be done around a house? What chores do you help with at home?*

Source: Frank Asch, *Country Pie*. New York: Greenwillow, 1979.

# COMMUNITIES HAVE HISTORIES

*Everybody says it was something to see how fast that town grew. All those people moving in and houses going up.*

Pattie Frances Ridley Jones
in *Childtimes*

# . . . *If You Lived at the Time of the Great San Francisco* EARTHQUAKE

**by Ellen Levine**

*After the gold rush, San Francisco was one of the fastest growing cities in the United States. It seemed as if nothing could stop its growth. Then, at 5:12 in the morning on April 18, 1906, a huge earthquake rocked the city. The earthquake lasted less than a minute, but it caused fires that burned for three days. Most of the city was destroyed. What was it like for the people who lived through this disaster? In this selection Ellen Levine answers some questions you might have about life at the time of the San Francisco earthquake.*

## What did San Francisco look like after the earthquake?

Everything was a mess! There were cracks in the streets that looked like giant zigzags. If you stood in one, it might be as high as your waist.

Telephone and electric wires had snapped and were hanging down from the poles. Cable car tracks that were in the ground were suddenly sticking up like huge, bent paper clips. And trolley car tracks lay twisted in the street.

Some trees had been pulled up by the roots. Branches were cracked and scattered around.

Chimneys had broken off rooftops throughout the city. Some chimneys had fallen inside homes, others were lying in the streets. In parts of the city, whole buildings had **collapsed**.

Walls of the new **city hall** building had fallen down. The dome was left standing on top of steel **pillars**. It had been the largest building in the state of California. After the earthquake, it looked like a skeleton.

**collapsed:** fallen

**city hall:** main government building for a city

**pillars:** posts holding up a building

88

The front wall of one hotel fell off completely, and the bedrooms looked like rooms in a doll's house. Can you imagine sitting in your bed and looking out at the street—with no windows in between!

Some buildings that were three or four stories high sank almost all the way into cracks in the ground. One nine-year-old girl remembered that her father took her out of their house through the attic window right onto the street.

Houses moved forward, backward, or sideways. If you went to bed on April 17th on one side of the street, you might have gotten up on April 18th across the street.

After the quake, one man climbed to the top of a hill and looked down on the city. From up high, people in the streets looked as if they were "running about like . . . excited insects."

Throughout San Francisco, water pipes had been broken by the earthquake. In some places, water was spurting up from the ground.

A cloud of dust filled the air. At times it was as thick as fog, and you couldn't see your hand in front of you. As the fires spread, there was smoke everywhere. It made your throat feel scratchy and your eyes itch.

Saddest of all was the sight of wounded or dead people and animals lying in the streets.

## What did people do when the quake struck?

It was a little after five o'clock in the morning when the earthquake struck, and most people were asleep. It was a frightening way to wake up. Many people were so **stunned** that they ran straight out into the streets.

When they got outside, they realized that they were in their pajamas and nightgowns! Some didn't care and just stayed outside until the earth stopped shaking. Many people didn't take the time to put on shoes, and that was dangerous—there was broken glass all over the ground.

stunned: surprised; shocked

89

One man was seen running down the street with his pants on backward, his suspenders hanging down the front, and his shoes unlaced.

Another man was wearing his top hat and his fancy evening tailcoat. Underneath the coat, all he had on was his long underwear!

These people may have looked silly, but they were lucky to be alive and outside.

A man named David Frazier was sleeping in a folding bed. When the earthquake hit, the bed snapped closed and he was trapped inside, bent over like a jackknife. He could hardly breathe, and was rescued just in time by a police officer who helped him to safety.

### What did the earthquake feel like?

Most people woke up at 5:12 in the morning because their beds were bumping and sliding around their rooms. It was some way to start the day!

Frank Ames said he felt as if he was in an elevator going down fast, sinking.

Anna Amelia Holshouser said she "danced" all the time she was trying to get dressed. Her legs kept bending and straightening, and she found herself jumping up and falling all around the room.

Colonel Mullally said it felt as if two invisible giants were wrestling under the hotel where he was staying.

One woman's house moved four feet down the road and then bumped along the ground for a while. She said she felt "like corn in a popper."

### How did people keep their spirits up?

It wasn't easy after an earthquake that shook up your world, and then fires that burned down your city. But the people of San Francisco did many things to cheer themselves up.

If a family had saved their piano from the flames, at night everyone would gather in the street and sing. The music drowned out the sounds of the crackling fires, the falling walls, and the dynamiting.

People also tried to keep their sense of humor. Sometimes they cracked jokes as they walked through the streets carrying their bundles. One man put down the heavy suitcase he was carrying, sat on it, and began to play his banjo. From where he sat, he could see the fires burning all over the city. When he began to sing, he picked the perfect song. It was called "There'll Be a Hot Time in the Old Town Tonight!"

People told jokes about the tents they lived in, the food they ate, and anything else you might think of.

The outdoor kitchens were a favorite place to put up signs.

One sign on a street kitchen said:
MAKE THE BEST OF IT—
FORGET THE REST OF IT.

Many people put signs on their tents. They said silly things, such as:
RING THE BELL FOR LANDLADY, or
ROOMS FOR RENT, or
ALL SHOOK UP!

When the quake was over and the fires were out, people began to rebuild the city. And they kept on putting up signs. On the wall of one new building were the words:
FIRST TO SHAKE
FIRST TO BURN
FIRST TO TAKE
ANOTHER NEW TURN!

*San Franciscans rebuilt their city quickly. Another earthquake struck San Francisco on October 17, 1989, but it was not as bad as the one in 1906. Some of the older neighborhoods were damaged. Luckily, all of the newer buildings had been built especially to survive earthquakes.*

Source: Ellen Levine, *. . . If You Lived at the Time of the Great San Francisco Earthquake*. New York: Scholastic, 1987.

# San Francisco
### by Langston Hughes

*San Francisco was completely rebuilt after the earthquake that you read about on pages 88–91. Today some people say that San Francisco is the prettiest city in the United States. It is surrounded by the beautiful waters of San Francisco Bay and the Pacific Ocean. Colorful houses sit on streets that wind up and down steep hills like a roller coaster. Two beautiful bridges connect the city to its neighboring communities. There are more than 100 parks, lots of tall buildings, and flowers everywhere. Many people have written about San Francisco's beauty. One of them is the poet, Langston Hughes. Here are two of his poems. What features does he write about?*

## City: San Francisco

In the morning the city
Spreads its wings
Making a song
In stone that sings.

In the evening the city
Goes to bed
Hanging lights
About its head.

## Trip: San Francisco

I went to San Francisco.
I saw the bridges high
Spun across the water
Like cobwebs in the sky.

*Many cities in the United States have interesting or beautiful features. Chicago and New York are famous for their skyscrapers. Washington, D.C., and Philadelphia have many historic places. Denver and Salt Lake City are near the snow-capped Rocky Mountains. What is special about your community?*

Source: *America Forever Now.* New York: Crowell, 1968.

# Bringing the Rain to Kapiti Plain

## A Nandi Tale Retold by Verna Aardema

*Nairobi is a growing city with industries and modern buildings. But most people in Kenya live in rural areas. For example, many Nandi people are herders who raise cattle and farm for a living on Kenya's Kapiti [Kə pē′ tē] Plain. They need rain for their animals. Often there are droughts [draut], or long periods without any rain. Is there anything people can do to make it rain? Nandi people tell this tale about how a herdsman named Ki-pat once ended a terrible drought. Verna Aardema has retold the story to give it the rhythm of the nursery rhyme "The House that Jack Built." How does Ki-pat bring rain?*

This is the great
  Kapiti Plain,
All fresh and green
  from the African rains—
A sea of grass for the
  ground birds to nest in,
And patches of shade for
  wild creatures to rest in;
With **acacia trees** for
  giraffes to **browse** on,
And grass for the herdsmen
  to pasture their cows on.

**acacia trees:** trees with small leaves and clusters of flowers

**browse:** to feed or nibble

But one year the rains
  were so very **belated**,
That all of the big wild
  creatures **migrated**.
Then Ki-pat helped to end
  that terrible drought—
And this story tells
  how it all came about!
This is the cloud,
  all heavy with rain,
That shadowed the ground
  on Kapiti Plain.
This is the grass,
  all brown and dead,
That needed the rain
  from the cloud overhead—
The big, black cloud,
  all heavy with rain,
That shadowed the ground
  on Kapiti Plain.
These are the cows,
  all hungry and dry,
Who mooed for the rain
  to fall from the sky;
To green-up the grass,
  all brown and dead,
That needed the rain
  from the cloud overhead—
The big, black cloud,
  all heavy with rain,
That shadowed the ground
  on Kapiti Plain.

This is Ki-pat,
  who watched his herd
As he stood on one leg,
  like the big stork bird;
Ki-pat, whose cows
  were so hungry and dry,
They mooed for the rain
  to fall from the sky;
To green-up the grass,
  all brown and dead,
That needed the rain
  from the cloud overhead—
The big, black cloud,
  all heavy with rain,
That shadowed the ground
  on Kapiti Plain.

**belated:** late

**migrated:** traveled
to another place

This is the eagle
  who dropped a feather,
A feather that helped
  to change the weather.
It fell near Ki-pat,
  who watched his herd
As he stood on one leg,
  like the big stork bird;
Ki-pat, whose cows
  were so hungry and dry,
They mooed for the rain
  to fall from the sky;
To green-up the grass,
  all brown and dead,
That needed the rain
  from the cloud overhead—
The big, black cloud,
  all heavy with rain,
That shadowed the ground
  on Kapiti Plain.
This is the arrow
  Ki-pat put together,
With a slender stick
  and an eagle feather;
From the eagle who happened
  to drop a feather,

A feather that helped
  to change the weather.
It fell near Ki-pat,
  who watched his herd
As he stood on one leg,
  like the big stork bird;
Ki-pat, whose cows
  were so hungry and dry,
They mooed for the rain
  to fall from the sky;
To green-up the grass,
  all brown and dead,
That needed the rain
  from the cloud overhead—
The big, black cloud,
  all heavy with rain,
That shadowed the ground
  on Kapiti Plain.
This is the bow,
  so long and strong,
And strung with a string,
  a leather **thong**;
A bow for the arrow
  Ki-pat put together,
With a slender stick
  and an eagle feather;
From the eagle who happened
  to drop a feather,
A feather that helped
  to change the weather.
It fell near Ki-pat,
  who watched his herd
As he stood on one leg,
  like the big stork bird;
Ki-pat, whose cows
  were so hungry and dry,

thong: narrow
  strip of leather

They mooed for the rain
  to fall from the sky;
To green-up the grass,
  all brown and dead,
That needed the rain
  from the cloud overhead—
The big, black cloud,
  all heavy with rain,
That shadowed the ground
  on Kapiti Plain.
This was the shot
  that pierced the cloud
And loosed the rain
  with thunder LOUD!
A shot from the bow,
  so long and strong,
And strung with a string,
  a leather thong;

A bow for the arrow
  Ki-pat put together,
With a slender stick
  and an eagle feather;
From the eagle who happened
  to drop a feather,
A feather that helped
  to change the weather.
It fell near Ki-pat,
  who watched his herd
As he stood on one leg,
  like the big stork bird;
Ki-pat, whose cows
  were so hungry and dry,
They mooed for the rain
  to fall from the sky;
To green-up the grass,
  all brown and dead,
That needed the rain
  from the cloud overhead—
The big, black cloud,
  all heavy with rain,
That shadowed the ground
  on Kapiti Plain.
So the grass grew green,
  and the cattle fat!
And Ki-pat got a wife
  and a little Ki-pat—
Who tends the cows now,
  and shoots down the rain,
When black clouds shadow
  Kapiti Plain.

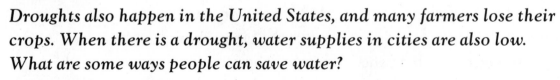

*Droughts also happen in the United States, and many farmers lose their crops. When there is a drought, water supplies in cities are also low. What are some ways people can save water?*

Source: Verna Aardema, *Bringing the Rain to Kapiti Plain*. New York: Dial, 1981.

# Down in a Coal Mine

## Folk Song

*Many American folk songs are work songs. They are the songs people sang to keep up their spirits while they were doing hard, backbreaking work. This song comes from the Monongahela Valley in Pennsylvania. It has been sung by coal miners for many years. What do you think it would be like to work underground, never seeing daylight?*

Source: Carl Carnerm, *America Sings.* New York: Knopf, 1942.

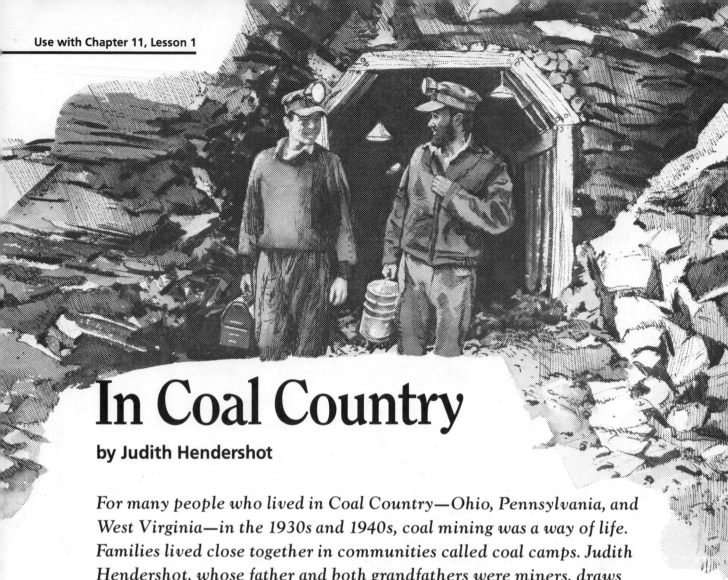

# In Coal Country

## by Judith Hendershot

*For many people who lived in Coal Country—Ohio, Pennsylvania, and West Virginia—in the 1930s and 1940s, coal mining was a way of life. Families lived close together in communities called coal camps. Judith Hendershot, whose father and both grandfathers were miners, draws from her parents' memories of a coal camp called Willow Grove to write this book. What was it like to grow up in a coal-mining community?*

Papa dug coal from deep in the earth to earn a living. He dressed for work when everyone else went to bed. He wore faded **denims** and steel-toed shoes and he walked a mile to his job at the mine every night. He carried a silver lunch bucket and had a light on his miner's hat. It was important work. He was proud to do it.

**denims:** jeans

In the morning I listened for the whistle that signaled the end of the **hoot-owl shift**. Sometimes I walked up the run to meet Papa. He was always covered with **grime** and dirt, but I could see the whites of his eyes smiling at me. He let me carry his silver lunch bucket.

**hoot-owl shift:** night working time

**grime:** greasy dirt

When we got home, Mama took the number three tub from where it hung on the back porch and filled it with water heated on the huge iron stove. She **draped** a blanket across one corner of the kitchen and Papa washed off the coal dust. We got a bath only on Saturdays, but Papa had one every day. Then Papa went to bed and we went to school.

**draped:** hung

We lived in a place called the Company Row. The ten white houses sat in a straight line. They were built by the people who owned the Black Diamond Mine. Two miners' families lived side by side in each two-story house. Seventy-five children lived and played there in the Row. We had many friends.

Outside, our houses never looked clean or painted. Coal was burned in the furnaces to heat the houses and in the stoves to cook the food. The stove fires sent smoke and soot up the chimneys. The smoke had a **disagreeable** smell, and something in it made the paint peel off the houses. Tiny specks of soot floated out and covered everything.

**disagreeable:** bad

Our coal camp was called Willow Grove. The houses were **huddled** in a **hollow** between two softly rising hills. In the spring the hills were covered with **lady's-slippers** and yellow and white violets. Mama always had a jar of spring flowers on the kitchen table. Weeping willow trees lined the banks of the creek that flowed behind the Company Row.

**huddled:** grouped closely together
**hollow:** a small valley
**lady's-slippers:** flowers with a petal that looks like a shoe

The water in the creek was often black. The coal was dragged out of the mine in small cars pulled by mules. Then it was sent up into a tall building called the tipple, where it was sorted and washed. The water that washed the coal ran into the creek, and the dust from the coal turned it black as night.

Papa sometimes worked at the picking table on the tipple to sort out rocks from the good coal. After it was sorted, the good coal was dumped into railroad cars waiting under the tipple. The rest of the stone and dirt was hauled away to a gob pile. There were gob piles all over Willow Grove. The kids from the Row ran to the tops of the piles to play king of the mountain.

Sometimes a gob pile caught fire. It **smouldered** for a long time, maybe for days, and it smelled awful. When the fire went out, the stone and ash that was left was called red dog. Our roads were made of the sharp red-dog stone.

**smouldered:** burned and smoked with little or no flame

Trains moved the coal in cars from the mine to power plants and steel mills on the Ohio River. The train tracks ran alongside the Company Row. We watched from the porch swing as the **engineer** worked his **levers** to guide the train, blowing clouds of hot white steam on the tracks. One engine pushed and another pulled as many as one hundred cars at a time. The houses shook as the trains rumbled by.

**engineer:** person who drives a train
**levers:** handles

The coal cars moved all through the day and into the night. Sometimes in the middle of the night we heard the clang of steel as the cars were **hitched** to the engine. Often the load was too much for the engine. It groaned. The tracks creaked. The wheels screeched as the brakeman spread sand on the rails to get the cars moving. Then the train began to move very slowly, and we could hear the wheels straining a slow "Chug-a-chug, chug-a-chug." Later in the distance, the engine's whistle moaned a familiar cry. "Whoo-whoo."

**hitched:** attached

In the morning we took buckets and gathered the lumps of coal that had rolled off the cars in the struggle the night before.

The **vibration** of the trains often made the rails on the tracks come apart. When that happened, the paddy man came to repair the tracks. He rode a **flatcar**, which he pedaled by himself. While he worked to replace the **spikes** in the rails, the paddy man sang:

*"Paddy on the railroad,*
*Paddy on the sea.*
*Paddy ripped his pants,*
*And he blamed it on me."*

Mama worked hard like Papa. She planted our garden and she canned vegetables for the winter. She stored her quart jars of beans and tomatoes and peas in the **earthen** room in the cellar. Every other day Mama baked her special rye bread in the oven of the iron stove. We often ate the bread right out of the oven with fried potatoes and sliced tomatoes.

Washing the clothes was a long, hard job. We carried the wash water from the pump down by the creek. Mama heated the water in a copper boiler on her huge stove. She scrubbed the clothes on a washboard with a stiff brush. Her hands were red and wrinkled when she was finished.

In the summer, when it was hot, the Company Row kids often climbed the hills above the grove. We cooled ourselves by standing under Bernice Falls. The water flowed from a natural spring on the **ridge** above. It was cool and clean and it tasted so sweet.

We walked the red-dog road to the Company Store. Anything the miners' families needed, from matches to **pongee** dresses, could be found there. Every payday Papa treated us to an **Eskimo Pie.**

**vibration:** shaking

**flatcar:** railroad car with a flat platform and no sides
**spikes:** large, heavy nails

**earthen:** made of baked clay

**ridge:** a long, narrow, raised strip of land

**pongee:** a soft, thin cloth made of silk
**Eskimo Pie:** vanilla ice cream bar covered with chocolate

The Company Row kids played hopscotch in the dirt. Our favorite game was **mumbletypeg**. In the evenings we built bonfires along the creek and roasted potatoes on willow sticks.

In the autumn the hills were ablaze with color. We gathered hickory nuts and butternuts and dragged them home in burlap sacks. Papa shelled them and spread them on the porch roof to dry. Mama used the nutmeats in cookies at holiday time.

In the winter we climbed from the hollow to Baker's Ridge. Our sleds were made from leftover tin used for roofs, and we rode them down through the woods by moonlight. When the black creek was frozen, we shared a few skates and everyone took a turn. When we got home, we hung our wet clothes over the stove to dry and warmed ourselves in Mama's kitchen.

Christmas in the row was the best time of the year. Papa cut a fresh tree up on the ridge, and we pulled it home on a tin sled. Mama placed a candle on the end of each branch. The tree was lighted once, on Christmas Eve. Papa spent the whole day **basting** the roast goose for Mama. Our stockings bulged with tangerines and nuts and hard cinnamon candies. The house smelled of Christmas tree and roast goose and all the good things that Mama had made. No whistle called Papa to the mine. Everything felt so special. And it was.

**mumbletypeg:** a game in which players try to throw a knife so the blade sticks in the ground

**basting:** adding a sauce to food while roasting

*Coal is still an important fuel. But the burning of coal causes a lot of air pollution. There are special methods to help this problem, but they cost a lot of money and they don't stop the pollution completely. Today people are looking for better ways to burn coal more cleanly and cheaply. As natural resources such as petroleum and natural gas get used up, we may need to depend on coal more and more in the future. This will keep coal towns like Willow Grove from disappearing.*

Source: Judith Hendershot, *In Coal Country.* New York: Knopf, 1987.

# Childtimes

## by Eloise Greenfield and Lessie Jones Little

*You have read about how Pittsburgh changed. If your parents or grandparents grew up in Pittsburgh, they might remember a city that is different from the one today. In the book Childtimes, three generations of one family—a grandmother, mother, and daughter—write about their childhoods. Some of their memories are about the town they knew while growing up—Parmele, North Carolina. Read what each woman remembers about Parmele. How and why did Parmele change?*

### Pattie Frances Ridley Jones
Born in Bertie County, North Carolina,
December 15, 1884

Towns build up around work, you know. People go and live where they can find jobs. And that's how Parmele got started.

At first, it was just a junction, a place where two railroads crossed. Two Atlantic Coast Line railroads, one running between Rocky Mount and Plymouth, and one running between Kinston and Weldon. Didn't too many people live around there then, and those that did were pretty much spread out.

Well, around 1888, a **Yankee** named Mr. Parmele came down from New York and looked the place over, and he saw all those big trees and decided to start a lumber company. Everybody knew what that meant. There were going to be jobs! People came from everywhere to get work. Was right little at that time, too little to know what was going on, but everybody says it was something to see how fast that town grew. All those people moving in and houses going up. They named the town after the man who made the jobs, and they called it *Pomma-lee.*

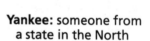

**Yankee:** someone from a state in the North

The lumber company hired a whole lot of people. They hired workers to lay track for those little railroads they call tram roads that they were going to run back and forth between the town and the woods. They hired lumberjacks to chop the trees down and cut them up into logs, and load them on the tram cars. They hired men to build the mill and put the machinery in, and millworkers to run the machines that would cut the logs into different sizes and dry them and make them nice and smooth. . . .

Well, after a good many years—about eighteen, I guess—the mill had to be closed down. Just about all of those great big trees were gone. Mr. Parmele moved his lumber mill away, to South Carolina if I remember right, and that didn't leave too many jobs in our town. A lot of people left, a lot of people. They moved to other places, looking for work.

## Lessie Blanche Jones Little
Born in Parmele, North Carolina,
October 1, 1906

I used to hear Papa and Mama and their friends talking about the lumber mill that had been the center of life in Parmele before I was born, but there wasn't any mill when I was growing up. The only thing left of it was the sawdust from all the wood they had sawed there. The sawdust was about a foot thick on the land where the mill had been. I used to love to walk on it. It was spongy, and it made me feel like I was made of rubber. I'd take my shoes off and kind of bounce along on top of it. But that was all that was left of the mill.

My Parmele was a train town. The life of my town moved around the trains that came in and out all day long. About three hundred people lived in Parmele, most of them black. . . .

Most of the men and women in Parmele earned their living by farming. Some did other things like working at the tobacco factory in Robersonville, but most worked on the farms that were all around in the area, white people's farms usually. When I was a little girl, they earned fifty cents a day, a farm day, sunup to sundown, plus meals. After they got home, they had all their own work to do, cooking and cleaning, laundry, chopping wood for the woodstove, and shopping.

I used to love to go shopping with Mama. There was so much to see downtown. When people started getting cars, the only gasoline pump in town was down there. There were stores, four or five stores, where you could buy clothes, or yard goods, or groceries, or hardware, and the post office was in the corner of one store. . . .

Parmele had trains coming in and going out all day long. Passenger trains and **freight trains**. There was always so much going on at the station that I wouldn't know what to watch. People were changing trains and going in and out of the cafe and the restaurant. They came from big cities like New York and Chicago and Boston, and they were all wearing the latest styles. Things were being unloaded, like furniture and trunks and plows and cases of fruit and crates of clucking chickens, or a puppy. . . .

**freight trains:** trains that carry goods

The train station was a gathering place, too. A lot of people went there to relax after they had finished their work for the day. They'd come downtown to pick up their mail, or buy a newspaper, and then they'd just stand around laughing and talking to their friends. And on Sundays fellas and their girls would come all the way from other towns, just to spend the afternoon at the Parmele train station.

## Eloise Glynn Little Greenfield
Born in Parmele, North Carolina,
May 17, 1929

I grew up in Washington, D.C. Every summer we took a trip down home. Down home was Parmele.

To get ready for our trip, Daddy would spend days working on our old car, putting it in shape to go on the road, and Mama would wash and iron all of our clothes. Then everything would be packed in the tan leather suitcase and the black cardboard suitcase, and we'd be ready to go.

Mama and Daddy would sit in the front with Vedie in Mama's lap, and Wilbur, Gerald, and I sat in the back with our legs on top of the suitcases. This was before cars had trunks. Or radios. Or air conditioners or heaters. And there were no superhighways. The **speed limit** was forty-five miles an hour, and we went thirty-five to keep from straining the car.

**speed limit:** how fast or slow cars are allowed to go

It was an eight-hour trip to Norfolk, Virginia, where we always went first. Grandma Pattie Ridley Jones and Grandpa had moved there by that time, and we'd spend about a week with them, then go on to Parmele for another week. . . .

By the time of my visits there, only a few trains were still passing through. My Parmele wasn't a train town or a mill town. It was a quiet town. Chinaberry trees and pump water and tree swings and figs and fat, **pulpy** grapes on the vine. People saying "hey" instead of "hi," the way they did in Washington, *hey-ey*, sending their voices up, then down, softly, singing it through their noses. Parmele was me running from the chickens when I was little, riding around the yard in a goat-pulled cart, sitting on the porch and letting people going by in their cars wave at me, reading in the rocking chair, taking long walks to the gas station for soda pop with the children of Mama's and Daddy's childtime friends. Parmele was uncles and aunts and cousins. And Granny. And Pa.

**pulpy:** juicy

*Parmele was a lumber mill town, a train town, then a quiet town. Do you know what your town or city was like long ago, and how it has changed?*

Source: Eloise Greenfield and Lessie Jones Little, *Childtimes*. New York: HarperCollins, 1979.

# Familytimes

**poems by Lessie Jones Little and Eloise Greenfield**

*In* Childtimes *you read about the memories of Eloise Greenfield and her mother, Lessie Jones Little. Both women have also written poetry. In* Children of Long Ago, *Lessie Jones Little imagines what life was like for children before she was born. In* Fambly Time, *Eloise Greenfield writes about a family today. How are the two poems alike? How are they different?*

## Children of Long Ago

The children who lived a long time ago
In little country towns
Ate picnics under spreading trees,
Played hopscotch on the cool dirt yards,
Picked juicy grapes from broad grapevines,
Pulled beets and potatoes from the ground,
Those children of long ago.
The children who lived a long time ago
In little country towns
Tromped to school on hard-frozen roads,
Warmed themselves by wood-burning stoves,
Ate supper by light from oil-filled lamps,
Built fancy snowmen dressed like clowns,
Those children of long ago.
The children who lived a long time ago
In little country towns
Decked themselves in their Sunday best,
Went to church and visited friends,
Sang happy songs with their mamas and papas,
Traveled through books for sights and sounds,
Those children of long ago.

## Fambly Time

When the Robinsons gather
Just before bed
The kids in pajamas
The homework's been read
It's time for the family
To have some fun
"It's fambly time!"
Says the littlest one
They come from work
They come from play
They get together
At the end of the day
For singing and guessing
And games of rhyme
For jokes and jacks
And pantomime
And the little one calls it
"Fambly time!"

*Think about these poems and about* Childtimes *on pages 103-106. What do you think Eloise Greenfield's childhood was like? How do you think she felt about her family?*

Sources: Lessie Jones Little, *Children of Long Ago*. New York: Philomel Books, 1988. Eloise Greenfield, *Night on Neighborhood Street*. New York: Dial Books, 1991.

# 50 Simple Things Kids Can Do to Save the Earth

## by John Javna and the EarthWorks Group

*The people of Pittsburgh all pitched in together to clean up the pollution caused by coal mining and factories. Marion Stoddart worked to clean up the river in her community in Massachusetts. There are things every person can do to protect the air, land, and water from pollution—even kids! The EarthWorks Group has printed a book called 50 Simple Things Kids Can Do to Save the Earth. You can read about air pollution below, and one of their suggestions for how you can make a difference.*

### AIR POLLUTION

#### THE OLD DAYS

Until about 150 years ago, the air was pure and clean—perfect for the people and animals of the earth to breathe.

#### FACTORIES

Then people started building factories. Those factories and many of the things they make, like cars, put a lot of harmful gases into the air. Then people started driving cars, which added more pollution to the air.

#### TODAY

Today the air is so polluted in some places that it's not always safe to breathe!

#### THE BROWN STUFF

Many cities around the world have air filled with a pollution called "smog." This is so strong in some places that the air, which should be a beautiful blue, actually looks brown.

## DOWN WITH POLLUTION!

Polluted air is not only bad for people and animals, but for trees and other plants, as well. And in some places it's even damaging farmers' crops—the food we eat. So it's very important for us to "clean up our act," and clean up the air we all breathe.

Everyone can help keep our air clean and safe. It's even fun! You can plant a tree, ride your bike, and even write a letter to a newspaper. For more ideas on how to clean up our air, keep reading!

## HANG ON TIGHT!
### Take a Guess.

**Which of these things shouldn't you do with balloons?**
**A) Celebrate a birthday    B) Decorate at a carnival**
**C) Feed them to whales**

Helium balloons! Big, bouncing, bobbing. . .Oops! One got away. There it goes, into the sky, getting smaller and smaller. . . until it's just a speck. Then you blink and it's gone.

Where do helium balloons go? Off into outer space? Not quite.

Actually, when they lose their helium, they come back to Earth. And that can be a problem for birds and other animals.

### Did You Know?

- When helium balloons are released, they are often blown by strong winds into the ocean. Even if the sea is hundreds of miles away, balloons can still land there.

**Answer: C. But we do it; helium balloons float to the ocean and get swallowed by whales!**

109

- The salt water in the ocean washes off a balloon's color, making it look clear.
- Sometimes sea creatures think balloons are food and eat them.
- Sea turtles, for example, eat jellyfish—which look and wiggle just like clear balloons. If a turtle makes a mistake and eats a balloon, the balloon can block its stomach. So the turtle can starve to death.
- Whales sometimes accidentally swallow balloons that are floating in the ocean. The balloons get stuck inside the whale's stomach, and can kill the creature!
- Another hazard: Silver metallic balloons (made of a material called Mylar) sometimes escape from people's hands and get caught in electric power lines. Then they cause the power to go out for many people.

### What You Can Do
- Try not to let go of your helium balloons.
- Tie them to your wristwatch, your shoe, your wrist, or anything handy.
- If your school plans to let lots of balloons into the air during a celebration, tell them about the dangers to sea animals. Most people don't realize that creatures can be harmed by balloons.

### See For Yourself
Test your strength: see how hard you need to pull to break a balloon in two. It probably won't be easy, and you may not be able to do it. That doesn't mean you're weak; it means balloons are made of strong material—another reason why they are so dangerous for sea creatures.

*What other ways can you think of to help protect your area? Why do you think it is especially important for children to learn about ways to stop pollution?*

Source: John Javna and the EarthWorks Group, *50 Simple Things Kids Can Do to Save the Earth*. Kansas City: Andrews and McMeel, 1990.

# COMMUNITIES HAVE GOVERNMENTS

*We are the children of the world. No matter who our parents are, where we live, or what we believe, treat us as equals. We deserve the best the world has to give.*

from *The Rights of the Child* by the United Nations

# Julio in the Lion's Den

## by Johanna Hurwitz

*You know that people vote in an election to choose government leaders to run their community. Students can also vote in an election to choose someone to lead their class. In the book* Class President, *Mr. Flores's fifth-grade class decides to hold an election to choose a class president. Julio Sanchez secretly wants to run, but he instead supports his best friend, Lucas. Lucas is running against Cricket Kaufman, the most popular girl in the class. Then, one day, Arthur Lewis breaks his glasses playing soccer. What does this have to do with the election? How does Julio find out what kind of president Cricket or Lucas would make?*

**O**n Monday, Arthur came to school with new glasses. Cricket came to class with a big poster that said, VOTE FOR CRICKET, THAT'S THE TICKET.

The election was going to be held on Friday. That meant there were only four days more to get ready. In the meantime, they learned about how to make a **nomination** and how to **second it**. It was going to be a really serious election.

At lunch, Cricket took out a bag of miniature chocolate bars and gave them out to her classmates.

**nomination:**
suggestion of a candidate, or someone who is running for office

**second it:** support it

---

112

Julio took his and ate it. But it didn't mean he was going to vote for Cricket. He wondered if there was anything Lucas could give out that was better than chocolate. Nothing was better than chocolate!

"If you're going to run against Cricket, we've got to get to work," Julio told Lucas on their way home. Julio wasn't very good at making posters, as Cricket and Zoe were, but he was determined to help his friend.

The next morning, a new poster appeared in Mr. Flores's classroom. It said, DON'T BUG ME. VOTE FOR LUCAS COTT. Julio had made it.

Before lunch, Mr. Flores read an announcement from the principal. "From now on, there is to be no more soccer playing in the school yard at lunchtime."

"No more soccer playing?" Julio called out. "Why not?"

Mr. Flores looked at Julio. "If you give me a moment, I'll explain. Mr. Herbertson is concerned about accidents. Last week, Arthur broke his glasses. Another time, someone might be injured more seriously."

Julio was about to call out again, but he remembered just in time and raised his hand.

"Yes, Julio," said Mr. Flores.

"It's not fair to make us stop playing soccer just because someone *might* get hurt. Someone might fall down walking to school, but we still have to come to school every day."

Julio didn't mean to be funny, but everyone started to laugh. Even Mr. Flores smiled.

"There must be other activities to keep you fellows busy at lunchtime," he said. "Is soccer the only thing you can do?"

Lucas raised his hand. "I don't like jumping rope," he said when the teacher called on him.

All the girls giggled at that.

"You could play jacks," suggested Cricket. Everyone knew it wasn't a serious possibility, though.

"Couldn't we tell Mr. Herbertson that we want to play soccer?" asked Julio.

"You could make an **appointment** to speak to him, if you'd like," said Mr. Flores. "He might change his decision if you convince him that you are right."

"Lucas and I will talk to him," said Julio. "Right, Lucas?"

"Uh, sure," said Lucas, but he didn't look too sure.

The principal, Mr. Herbertson, spoke in a loud voice and had eyes that seemed to bore right into your head when he looked at you. Julio had been a little bit afraid of Mr. Herbertson since the very first day of kindergarten. Why had he offered to go to his office and talk to him?

Mr. Flores sent Julio and Lucas down to the principal's office with a note, but the principal was out of the office at a meeting.

"You can talk to him at one o'clock," the secretary said.

At lunch, Cricket had more chocolate bars. This time, she had pasted labels on them and printed in tiny letters, *Cricket is the ticket*. She must be spending her whole allowance on the **campaign**, Julio thought.

After a few more days of free chocolate bars, everyone in the class would be voting for Cricket.

At recess, the girls were jumping rope. You could fall jumping rope, too, Julio thought.

Back in the classroom, Julio wished he could think up some good arguments to tell the principal. He looked over at Lucas. Lucas didn't look very good. Maybe he was coming down with the flu.

Just before one o'clock, Julio had a great idea. Cricket was always saying she wanted to be a lawyer. She always knew what to say in class. Julio figured she'd know just what to do in the principal's office, too. He raised his hand.

"Mr. Flores, can Cricket go down to Mr. Herbertson's office with Lucas and me? She's running for president, so she should stick up for our class."

"Me?" Cricket said. "I don't care if we can't play soccer."

**appointment:** date to meet or see someone

**campaign:** time before an election when candidates try to win votes

114

"Of course," teased Lucas. "You couldn't kick a ball if it was glued to your foot."

"Cricket," said Mr. Flores, "even if you don't want to play soccer, others in the class do. If you are elected, you will be president of the whole class, not just the girls. I think going to the meeting with Mr. Herbertson will be a good **opportunity** for you to **represent** the class."

**opportunity:** chance
**represent:** speak for

So that was why at one o'clock Julio, Lucas, and Cricket Kaufman went downstairs to the principal's office.

Mr. Herbertson **gestured** for them to sit in the chairs facing his desk. Cricket looked as pale as Lucas. Maybe she, too, was coming down with the flu.

**gestured:** showed with hands

Julio waited for the future first woman President of the United States to say something, but Cricket didn't say a word. Neither did Lucas. Julio didn't know what to do. They couldn't just sit here and say nothing.

Julio took a deep breath. If Cricket or Lucas wasn't going to talk, he would have to do it. Julio started right in.

"We came to tell you that it isn't fair that no one can play soccer at recess just because Arthur Lewis broke his eyeglasses. Anybody can have an accident. He could have tripped and broken them getting on the school bus." Julio was amazed that so many words had managed to get out of his mouth. No one else said anything, so he went on. "Besides, a girl could fall jumping rope," said Julio. "But you didn't say that they had to stop jumping rope."

"I hadn't thought of that," said Mr. Herbertson.

Cricket looked alarmed. "Can't we jump rope anymore?" she asked.

"I didn't mean that you should make the girls stop jumping rope," Julio went on quickly. He stopped to think of a better example. "Your chair could break while you're sitting on it, Mr. Herbertson," he said.

Mr. Herbertson adjusted himself in his chair. "I certainly hope not," he said, smiling. "What is your name, young man?"

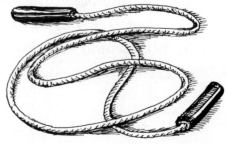

"Julio. Julio Sanchez." He pronounced it in the Spanish way with the J having an H sound.

"You have a couple of brothers who also attended this school, Julio, don't you?" asked the principal. "Nice fellows. I remember them both."

Julio smiled. He didn't know why he had always been afraid of the principal. He was just like any other person.

"Julio," Mr. Herbertson went on, "you've got a good head on your shoulders, just like your brothers. You made some very good points this afternoon. I think I can arrange things so that there will be more teachers **supervising** the yard during recess. Then you fellows can play soccer again tomorrow." He turned to Cricket. "You can jump rope if you'd rather do that," he said.

**supervising:** watching over

Cricket smiled. She didn't look so pale anymore.

Julio and Lucas and Cricket returned to Mr. Flores's classroom. "It's all arranged," said Cricket as soon as they walked in the door.

The class burst into cheers.

"Good work," said Mr. Flores.

Julio was proud that he had stood up to Mr. Herbertson. However, it wasn't fair that Cricket made it seem as if she had done all the work. She had hardly done a thing. For that matter, Lucas hadn't said anything, either. For a moment, Julio wished he hadn't offered to be Lucas's campaign **manager**. He wished he was the one running for class president. He knew he could be a good leader.

**manager:** person in charge

*Do you think Julio would make a good leader? Why? What happened in the principal's office that showed he might be a better class president than Cricket or Lucas? What qualities should a class president have? Who would you choose to be president of your class?*

Source: Johanna Hurwitz, *Class President*. New York: Scholastic, 1990.

# ...If You Were There When They Signed the Constitution

**by Elizabeth Levy**

*In 1787 leaders called delegates met in Philadelphia to write a plan of government for the new United States of America. This plan, called the Constitution, became the most important law of our country. What rules does the Constitution provide for choosing a President? Who makes the laws? What is the Bill of Rights? These are some of the questions you might have asked if you were there when the delegates signed the Constitution.*

## How did the delegates invent a President?

The men at Philadelphia knew first hand what it was like to be ruled by a king. They wanted to make sure that no one man would ever have as much power as a king.

But on the other hand, they had lived for twelve years under a system when there was no head of the government, and that hadn't worked very well.

At the Philadelphia **Convention** during the hot summer, they had invented a House of Representatives and a Senate to make up the laws. But what if the House and the Senate voted foolish laws? Who would stop them? Would we have to go through another revolution?

No, they wanted a government where there would be someone strong enough to "check" the House and Senate, but not so strong that he could make himself king. They wanted someone who could lead the country in

**convention:** formal meeting for a certain purpose

times of emergency and deal with the heads of other nations. They decided to call this person "President."

## What does the President do?

The President cannot make laws. Only Congress can make laws, but the President has to carry out the laws. And the President can suggest laws.

One of the most important things any government has to decide is when and if to go to war. The delegates believed this was too big a question for one person to decide. It seemed to them that kings were always going to war and sending people to their deaths.

The delegates made the President Commander in Chief of the Army, but the President can not declare war on another country. Only Congress can declare war.

## Who would be President?

The truth was that everyone in the room knew exactly who would be the first President. They had been looking at him all summer. It was George Washington.

But they knew Washington wouldn't live forever. Remember, they were inventing a new office: President. Who should pick the President?

They went round and round on this question. First they voted that the President should be picked by the Senate, but then they didn't like that.

James Wilson from Philadelphia kept arguing that the President should be elected by the people as a whole. This was a lot for the delegates to swallow. It was rare for anyone in Georgia to know anyone in Massachusetts. How would anyone ever know who would be the best President?

In the end the delegates made up an "electoral college." Although the electoral college is a strange and **complicated** system, James Wilson was right. Almost from the beginning, the President came to be seen as not just from one state, but as someone who has to **represent** all the people.

**complicated:** not simple

**represent:** speak or act for

118

### *Who would make the laws? Congress or the President?*

It takes both Congress and the President to make a law. There are a lot of checks and balances built into the system.

Suppose a member of Congress suggests a law making everyone eat peanut butter and mayonnaise sandwiches for lunch every day.

"That's crazy!" you might say. But how would you stop the law?

The delegates wanted to make sure that before any suggestion became a law it would have to go through many steps, and at each step it could be "checked" or stopped if it was a bad law.

An awful lot of people would have to like peanut butter and mayonnaise before having it for lunch became the law.

### *How are laws passed?*

A law begins with a **proposal** called a *bill*. Most bills can start in either the House of Representatives or the Senate, but before a bill becomes a law, both branches of Congress must vote for it.

**proposal:** suggestion

Then the President gets the bill. If he or she doesn't like it, the President can say no, or veto it. (*Veto* comes from the Latin word "forbid.")

But the President's veto doesn't have to be the end of a bill. Congress can pass a bill over the President's veto if two-thirds of both the House and the Senate think the bill should be a law.

Chances are that two-thirds of the Senators and two-thirds of the Representatives would not like peanut butter and mayonnaise, and this bill would never get to be a law.

### *Why did the delegates invent the Supreme Court?*

The delegates knew that there would need to be a court to decide fights between the states, and to decide

if any of the states were passing laws that went against the Constitution. They had been using the British court system and expected their judges to go on following that tradition.

They knew that there would have to be a whole system of Federal Courts with a Supreme Court at the top, but they left out many details about how the courts would work.

The courts would be another check against any one group getting too much power. But how do you get an independent court?

The delegates decided to let the President **nominate** the Justices for the Supreme Court. However, the Senate would have to agree with the President's choice, or the President would have to suggest someone else.

nominate: choose for office

### How can we change the Constitution?

The delegates wanted their Constitution to last. They wanted people in the future to have a way to change the government without having another revolution.

They wanted their new Constitution to be easier to change than the old Articles of Confederation, which had said that nothing could be changed unless every single state agreed.

The Constitution spells out two ways it can be changed. One way would be to make major changes and to call another convention. It would take two-thirds of the states to call one.

This method has never been used.

The second way is to amend the Constitution.

### What is an amendment?

An amendment is a specific change in the Constitution. There have been amendments to end slavery and to give women the vote. All in all we have approved only twenty-six amendments.

It is not easy to change the Constitution with an amendment. An amendment has to be approved by

two-thirds of both the Senate and the House of Representatives.

Then it is taken to the states, where it has to be voted on by either the state legislature or a special convention. Three-quarters of all the states must pass an amendment before it becomes part of the Constitution.

### What was missing from the Constitution?

There was no Bill of Rights in the original Constitution. A Bill of Rights protects you, the individual, from the power of your government. The idea of a Bill of Rights, a list of things that the government cannot do, goes way back in English history, back to 1215, when the English lords made King John sign the **Magna Carta**.

**Magna Carta:** "Great Charter" listing rights that landowners and church leaders demanded from King John

### What are some of the rights in a Bill of Rights?

One of the rights guaranteed in a Bill of Rights is freedom of religion. Under English rule many colonists did not enjoy freedom to **worship** as they pleased. When James Madison was a young man in Virginia, the Church of England was the colony's official church. Baptists and Methodists were often thrown into jail.

**worship:** pray to God

After the Revolution, the state government of Virginia declared that all people should be free to worship as they choose. They made freedom of religion part of their Bill of Rights. The Virginia Bill of Rights also said that all men were free and equal. It forbade cruel and unusual punishment. It gave all people the right to trial by jury.

Many other states copied the Virginia Bill of Rights into their own Constitutions.

*The Bill of Rights was added to the Constitution in 1791 as the first ten amendments. These rights protect certain freedoms of people, such as the right to say what you want, go where you want, and practice whatever religion you want. The Constitution is more than 200 years old. Many say that it has lasted so long because amendments allow it to change with the times.*

Source: Elizabeth Levy, *...If You Were There When They Signed the Constitution*. New York: Scholastic, 1987.

# The Rights of the Child
## by the United Nations

*In 1791 the Bill of Rights was added to the Constitution to protect certain rights and freedoms of people in the United States. In 1959 the United Nations adopted the Declaration of the Rights of the Child to protect certain rights for children all over the world. Here are the ten principles that make up the Declaration of the Rights of the Child. What rights do you think children should have?*

**Principle One:** We are the children of the world. No matter who our parents are, where we live, or what we believe, treat us as equals. We deserve the best the world has to give.

**Principle Two:** Protect us, so that we may grow in freedom and with **dignity**.

**dignity:** self-respect, or feeling of self-worth

**Principle Three:** Let us each be given a name, and have a land to call our own.

**Principle Four:** Keep us warm and **sheltered**. Give us food to eat and a place to play. If we are sick, nurse and comfort us.

**sheltered:** provided with a home

**Principle Five:** If we are handicapped in body or mind, treasure us even more and meet our special needs.

**Principle Six:** Let us grow up in a family. If we cannot be cared for by our own family, take us in and love us just the same.

**Principle Seven:** Teach us well, so that we may lead happy and useful lives. But let us play, so that we may also teach ourselves.

**Principle Eight:** In times of trouble, help us among the first. The future of the world depends on us.

**Principle Nine:** Protect us from **cruelty** and from those who would use us badly.

**cruelty:** causing suffering or pain

**Principle Ten:** Raise us with **tolerance**, freedom, and love. As we grow up, we, too, will **promote** peace and understanding throughout the world.

**tolerance:** ability to accept others
**promote:** work for

*Many children are lucky enough to be able to take these rights for granted. But there are many other children, especially those in poor countries, whose basic needs are not being met. The United Nations tries to help these children. It has saved millions of lives by providing food, water, medicine, and education to children in more than 120 countries.*

Source: *A Children's Chorus.* New York: Dutton, 1989.

# What Are You Figuring Now?
## A Story About Benjamin Banneker

### by Jeri Ferris

*In 1731 Benjamin Banneker was born on a farm in Maryland. While most of the other African Americans on the farm were enslaved, Benjamin and his family were free. He grew up to become a good farmer, but that wasn't enough for him. Banneker had a head for numbers. He studied as much math as he could on his own. Then, in 1771 he became friends with George Ellicott, who was studying to be a surveyor, a person who measures land. Banneker was able to use his math knowledge to help his friend survey, and to learn this skill at the same time. With Ellicott's books and instruments, Banneker taught himself astronomy, too. He spent years studying the sun, moon, stars, and planets through his telescope. When he was almost 60 years old, Benjamin Banneker got the chance to use what he had learned. Read the selection from the biography below to see how he helped to build the new capital city.*

By 1790, the revolutionary war had been over for 7 years and the Declaration of Independence was 14 years old, but the new United States still had no capital. So President George Washington chose a spot for the city right in the middle of the 13 states, in the woods overlooking the Potomac River. He chose Frenchman Pierre L'Enfant to plan just where the streets and buildings would look best, and he ordered the survey for the new city to begin in 1791.

The surveyor had to lay out the straight lines for the 10-square-mile city. He had to **plot** a perfect line running north and south using the stars, his instruments, his **astronomical clock**, and his **calculations**. Then he had to cross it with a perfect line running east and west. The United States Capitol was to be built on the hill where the two lines crossed.

**plot:** make a map of

**astronomical clock:** a clock that shows the position of stars in the sky

**calculations:** figures arrived at by doing math

Major Andrew Ellicott, George Ellicott's cousin, was chosen to be the chief surveyor. But Major Ellicott needed help. He needed someone who knew astronomy and surveying. He needed someone who knew math and figuring. He needed someone who knew clocks. In short, he needed Benjamin Banneker.

President Washington and Thomas Jefferson, the secretary of state, agreed that Benjamin Banneker was just the man to be the chief surveyor's chief assistant. Benjamin hoped to prove they were right.

He put aside his telescope and **drafting** tools, and he packed his best dark suit and white linen shirts. He added his quill pen, an ink bottle, and some paper, in case he had time to make notes for his **almanac**. Before he left, he asked his sisters and their husbands to look after his farm.

**drafting:** drawing or sketching

**almanac:** a book put out every year, with information about the weather and many other subjects

On a cold, rainy morning in early February 1791, when Benjamin was almost 60 years old, he and Major Ellicott set off on horseback to make camp in Alexandria, Virginia, about 40 miles away. They arrived, wet and cold, on the evening of February 7.

The next day, the two men rode to a hill outside the town to set up the **observation tent,** where Benjamin would work. Andrew Ellicott owned some of the finest astronomical instruments in the world, and Benjamin was to use them. He was in charge of the astronomical clock, three large telescopes, and many other tools used in surveying.

 At last the survey began. Andrew took his crew of men and began chopping down trees so he could lay out straight lines for the city. Benjamin set up the largest and best telescope so that it pointed through an opening in the roof of the tent. That night, he began his observations of the stars as they crossed a certain point in the sky. He recorded each observation, . . .

**observation tent:** a place from which to watch things

and drew the **base points** for the lines Andrew would lay the following day.

**base points:** starting points

When the stars faded, Benjamin had time for only a short nap. Soon he was up again to explain his figures to Andrew, to record observations of the sun, and to check the astronomical clock.

It rained a lot that spring, and it was cold at night in the tent. In fact, it was cold in the daytime, too, but Benjamin was too busy to mind. If he ever had a spare minute, which wasn't often, he would use the time to work on his almanac.

On March 12, Benjamin's name was in the newspaper. The *Georgetown Weekly Ledger* reported that Andrew Ellicott was "attended by *Benjamin Banniker* ...surveyor and astronomer." His name was spelled wrong again, but Benjamin carefully and proudly folded his copy of the newspaper and laid it aside with his notes.

That same month, Benjamin met the most famous man in the United States. President Washington himself came to visit the survey camp on March 28. Benjamin dressed in his best dark suit, his finest linen shirt, and a new three-cornered hat. He smiled when he heard someone in the crowd say that Mr. Banneker looked like Benjamin Franklin with brown skin.

When Benjamin bowed deeply before the tall president, he tried to feel as calm on the inside as he looked on the outside, but his heart felt like a runaway clock.

On April 15, Benjamin again dressed in his very best clothes. He stood with Andrew Ellicott and Pierre

L'Enfant as the first stone marker was placed at Jones's Point. This marked the first corner of the capital city.

By late spring, Benjamin had finished his figures. After working night and day, seven days a week, he was ready to return to his farm. Before he left, Benjamin looked at L'Enfant's plans for the new city. They showed streets laid out like a checkerboard, with wide avenues spreading out from the Capitol like the spokes of a wheel. They also included plenty of parks and fountains. Benjamin thought the plans were just right.

As he walked to his horse, Benjamin thought about his three months as the chief surveyor's chief assistant. He felt proud that he, Benjamin Banneker, had helped to lay out the capital city of the United States.

Benjamin stopped at the Ellicott's store on the way home to buy candles, ink, and paper. His neighbors saw him and hurried over to shake his hand and ask about his adventures.

Hours later, Benjamin shook the last hand and got back on his horse. In his bulging saddlebags were his suit, his notes, the newspaper with his name in it, and the new candles and ink from the store. Tucked away carefully was a brand-new, handsome book with three hundred blank pages of handmade paper. Benjamin planned to write his almanac on these fine pages.

At last he was home. When Benjamin opened the cabin door, he was greeted by the ticking of his wooden clock. The cabin was clean and neat. His sisters had taken good care of it and of his farm while he was gone.

*Later, Pierre L'Enfant had an argument with the city planners. He left the project and took the plans with him. Fortunately, Banneker was not only a good planner—he had a good memory as well! Banneker went on to help build Washington, D.C., which is still our capital today.*

Source: Jeri Ferris, *What Are You Figuring Now? A Story About Benjamin Banneker*. Minneapolis: Carolrhoda Books, 1988.

# Rise and Shine
## (Give Yourself a Chance)
### by Professor Rap

*In your textbook you read about many people who made a difference by helping their communities. This song says that everyone can make a difference and feel good about themselves. All you have to do is give yourself a chance. What does this song say about doing your best? Why is it important to be yourself?*

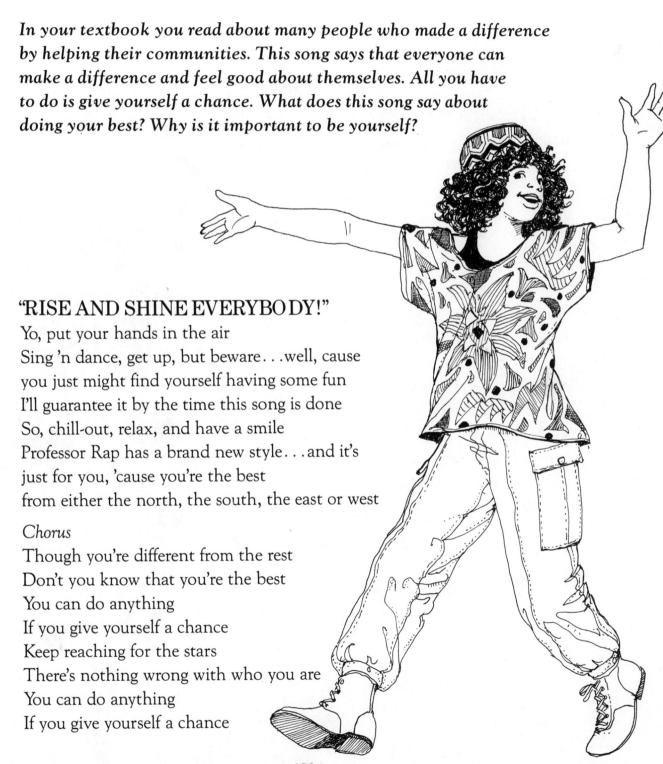

**"RISE AND SHINE EVERYBODY!"**
Yo, put your hands in the air
Sing 'n dance, get up, but beware...well, cause
you just might find yourself having some fun
I'll guarantee it by the time this song is done
So, chill-out, relax, and have a smile
Professor Rap has a brand new style...and it's
just for you, 'cause you're the best
from either the north, the south, the east or west

*Chorus*
Though you're different from the rest
Don't you know that you're the best
You can do anything
If you give yourself a chance
Keep reaching for the stars
There's nothing wrong with who you are
You can do anything
If you give yourself a chance

When I awake and open my eyes
I think good thoughts and then I rise
I like you, and I like me
We're just fine, and we'll always be...
Together...forever

Under sunny skies, through stormy weather
   (I'll be there for you)
You can count on me, I'll be nice to you
'Cause that's what true friends were meant to do

*Chorus*
We're all different from A to Z
That's what's fun...the variety
Eyes of blue, brown, hazel or green
Are the prettiest eyes that I've ever seen
Some people are fast, and others are slow
Being kind to all I know...
Will make me...feel good inside
Warm in my heart and in my mind

*Chorus*
Cheer up...pat yourself on the back
Yeah, it's about time you gave yourself a little slack
Try, and try, and try, and try again
You're bound to get what you want in the end
And I hope that you do much more than just listen
Set your goals, I mean it, go on a mission...
To be...exactly what you want to be
I'll accept you as you, as you accept me as me

*Chorus*
Breakin' it down into day-by-day
I like to work and I like to play
And I always want to do my best
Ya see, I'm good to me and all the rest...
Of you...You see, you're not like me
We're all unique and that's good you see

*Chorus*
Sing it Rap, go to Pro. Rap. *(repeat)*

*Chorus*
Now, I'm Professor Rap and I'm on your team, and
I'd like to help you raise your self esteem
Accept who you are, you're you for a reason
So just be yourself...it's you you should be pleasing
Be honest with people, and more important with
   yourself
Trust me, it's right, and good for mental health
So, if someone is different, or from another nation
Make a friend...better the next generation
(Peace!)

Source: Professor Rap, *Rise and Shine (Give Yourself a Chance)*. Utica, Michigan: Dalka Studios, 1991.

# INDEX BY *Category*

**Biographies and Autobiographies**

Childtimes, 103

What Are You Figuring Now? A Story About
   Benjamin Banneker, 124

**Folk Tales, Tall Tales, Legends, and Fables**

Bringing the Rain to Kapiti Plain, 93

Great Race, The, 34

John Henry, 21

Why We Have Dogs in Hopi Villages, 42

**Nonfiction Stories, Interviews, and
   Documents**

50 Simple Things Kids Can Do to Save the
   Earth, 108

. . . If You Lived at the Time of the Great San
   Francisco Earthquake, 88

. . . If You Sailed on the *Mayflower*, 47

. . . If You Were There When They Signed the
   Constitution, 117

Kwanzaa, 3

Rights of the

Child, The, 122

Working on an Assembly Line, 81

**Play**

Cross and Sword, 45

**Poems**

Before You Came This Way, 38

Children of Long Ago, 107

City: San Francisco, 92

Fambly Time, 107

Field, 86

Fourth, The, 2

In a Neighborhood in Los Angeles, 78

Picking Berries, 67

Rhyme-Time Fun, 64

Rudolph Is Tired of the City, 63

Sing a Song of People, 77

Trip: San Francisco, 92

**Songs**

City Blues, The, 80

Down in a Coal Mine, 97

In Good Old Colony Times, 50

Rhyme-Time Fun, 64

Rise and Shine (Give Yourself a Chance), 129

**Stories**

Best Town in the World, The, 52

House on Hillside La, The, 83

How Pizza Came to Queens, 68

In Coal Country, 98

Julio in the Lion's Den, 112

Ming Lo Moves the Mountain, 28

Mr. Griggs' Work, 18

Music, Music for Everyone, 12

My Best Friend, Mee-Yung Kim, 7

Patchwork Quilt, The, 71

Where the River Begins, 25

Yagua Days, 58

Before You Came This Way, 38
Best Town in the World, The, 52
Bringing the Rain to Kapiti Plain, 92

Children of Long Ago, 107
Childtimes, 103
City Blues, The 80
City: San Francisco, 92
Cross and Sword, 45

Down in a Coal Mine, 97

50 Simple Things Kids Can Do to Save the Earth,
    108
Fambly Time, 107
Field, 86
Fourth, The, 2

Great Race, The, 34

House on Hillside La, The, 83
How Pizza Came to Queens, 68
. . . If You Lived at the Time of the Great San
    Francisco Earthquake, 88
. . . If You Sailed on the *Mayflower,* 47
. . . If You Were There When They Signed the
    Constitution, 117
In a Neighborhood in Los Angeles, 78
In Coal Country, 98
In Good Old Colony Times, 50

John Henry, 21
Julio in the Lion's Den, 112

Kwanzaa, 3

Ming Lo Moves the Mountain, 28
Mr. Griggs' Work, 18

Music, Music for Everyone, 12
My Best Friend, Mee-Yung Kim, 7

Patchwork Quilt, The, 70
Picking Berries, 67
Rhyme-Time Fun, 64
Rights of the Child, The, 122
Rise and Shine (Give Yourself a Chance), 129
Rudolph Is Tired of the City, 63

Sing a Song of People, 77

Trip: San Francisco, 92

What Are You Figuring Now? A Story About
    Benjamin Banneker, 124
Where the River Begins, 25
Why We Have Dogs in Hopi Villages, 42
Working on an Assembly Line, 81

Yagua Days, 58

Aardema, Verna, 93
Alarcón, Francisco, X., 78
Asch, Frank, 86

Baylor, Byrd, 38, 52
Baylor, Byrd, with Hopi children, 42
Brooks, Gwendolyn, 63

Chocolate, Deborah M. Newton, 3

EarthWorks Group, The, and Javana, John, 108

Ferris, Jeri, 124
Fisher, Aileen, 67
Flournoy, Valerie, 71
Freeman, Dorothy, and MacMillan, Dianne, 7

Goble, Paul, 34
Green, Paul, 45
Greenfield, Eloise, and Little, Lessie Jones, 103, 107

Hendershot, Judith, 98
Hopi children, with Byrd Baylor, 42
Hughes, Langston, 92
Hurwitz, Johanna, 83, 112

Javana, John, and The EarthWorks Group, 108
Johnson, Neil, 81

Keats, Ezra Jack, 21

Lenski, Lois, 77
Levine, Ellen, 88
Levy, Elizabeth, 117
Little, Lessie Jones, and Greenfield, Eloise, 103, 107
Lobel, Arnold, 28
Locker, Thomas, 25

MacMillan, Dianne, and Freeman, Dorothy, 7
Martel, Cruz, 58
McGovern, Ann, 47
Medearis, Angela Shelf, 68

Rap, Professor, 129
Rylant, Cynthia, 18

Silverstein, Shel, 2

United Nations, 122

Williams, Vera B., 12

# INDEX BY *Subject*

## A

Architecture, 88-92, 124-128
Assembly line, 81-82
Aviles, Pedro Menéndez de, 45-46

## B

Ballads, 50
Banneker, Benjamin, 124-128
Bill of Rights, 117-121
Buffalo, 34

## C

Children, 7-17, 25-27, 52-76, 78-79, 83-85,
    103-106, 107-110, 112-116, 122-123
City life, 63, 77-79, 88-92, 124-128
Coal mining, 97-102
Constitution, United States, 117-121
Country life, 25-27, 52-57, 67-70, 86,k 93-96
Courts, 117-121

## E

Elections, 112-121
Exploring, 25-27

## F

Families, 3-17, 52-62, 67, 71-76, 78-79, 83-85,
    98-107, 122-123
Family get-togethers, 3-17, 50-60
Farming and herding, 68-70, 93-96
Fourth of July, 2

## G

Games, 64-66, 107
Government, 112-121

## H

Henry, John, 21-24
Heritage, 2-11, 34-50, 52-60, 64-66, 78-79, 93-96
Holidays, 2-11, 52-62, 98-102

## J

Jobs and working, 18-24, 68-70, 81-82, 97-106

## K

Kwanzaa, 3-6

## L

Laws and rules, 112-121
Leaders, 112-121
Los Angeles, 78-79
Lumbering, 103-106

## M

Mayflower, 47-49
Mexico, 78-79
Moving to a new home, 47-49, 83-85
Music, 12-17

## N

Nairobi, Kenya, 93-96
Natural environment, 25-32, 34-41, 58-62, 67, 86,
    88-91, 93-102, 108-110

## P

People, helping others, 12-17, 68-76, 88-91, 98-102
Picking fruit and vegetables, 67-70
Pilgrims, 47-50
Pollution, 98-102, 108-110
Post office, 18-20
Problem solving, 12-17, 28-32, 71-76
Puerto Rico, 58-62

## R

Railroads, 21-24, 103-106
Rights, 117-123
Rivers, 25-27
Rock paintings, 38-41

## S

San Francisco, 88-92
Self-esteem, 129-131
Service workers, 18-20
Small-town life, 42-44, 52-62, 98-107
St. Augustine, Florida, 45-46
Street rhymes, 64-66
Suburban life, 83-88

## T

Texas, 52-57
Theater, 45-46

## U

United Nations, 122-123
United States Constitution, 117-121

## W

Washington, D.C., 124-128
Washington, George, 117-121, 124-128
Work songs, 97

*(continued from copyright page)*

Excerpts from KWANZAA by Deborah M. Newton Chocolate. Copyright © 1990 by Childrens Press, Inc.

"En un barrio de Los Angeles"/"In a Neighborhood in Los Angeles" from CUERPO EN LLAMAS/BODY IN FLAMES by Francisco X. Alarcón. Copyright © 1990 by Francisco X. Alarcón. Reprinted by permission of Chronicle Books.

Excerpt and two illustrations from HOW PIZZA CAME TO QUEENS by Dayal Kaur Khalsa. Copyright © 1989 by Dayal Kaur Khalsa. Reprinted by permission of Clarkson N. Potter, Inc.

'In Good Old Colony Times" from THE FOLKSONGS OF NORTH AMERICA.

Scene 6 from The Official State Play of Florida CROSS AND SWORD *A Symphonic Drama* by Paul Green. Reprinted by permission of Samuel French Inc.

"Picking Berries" from OUT IN THE DARK AND DAYLIGHT by Aileen Fisher. Copyright © 1980 by Aileen Fisher. Used by permission of HarperCollins Publishers.

"The Fourth" from WHERE THE SIDEWALK ENDS by Shel Silverstein. Copyright © 1974 by Evil Eye Music, Inc. Reprinted by permission of HarperCollins Publishers.

"Rudolph is Tired of the City" from BRONZEVILLE BOYS AND GIRLS by Gwendolyn Brooks. Copyright © 1956 by Gwendolyn Brooks Blakely. Used by permission of HarperCollins Publishers.

Excerpt from CHILDTIMES *A Three-Generation Memoir* by Eloise Greenfield and Lessie Jones Little. Copyright © 1979 by Eloise Greenfield and Lessie Jones Little. Reprinted by permission of HarperCollins Publishers.

Excerpts from ...IF YOU SAILED ON THE MAYFLOWER by Ann McGovern. Copyright © 1969 by Ann McGovern. Reprinted by permission of Ann McGovern.

"Sing a Song of People" from THE LIFE I LIVE by Lois Lenski. Copyright © 1965 by The Lois Lenski Covey Foundation, Inc. Used by permission of The Lois Lenski Covey Foundation, Inc.

"Assembly-line Worker" from ALL IN A DAY'S WORK by Neil Johnson. Copyright © 1989 by Neil Johnson. By permission of Little, Brown and Company.

Excerpt from THE BEST TOWN IN THE WORLD by Byrd Baylor. Copyright © 1982 by Byrd Baylor. Reprinted with the permission of Charles Scribner's Sons, an imprint of Macmillan Publishing Company.

THE GREAT RACE by Paul Goble. Copyright © 1985 by Paul Goble. Reprinted with the permission of Bradbury Press, an affiliate of Macmillan, Inc.

Text of Chapter 7 "Julio in the Lion's Den" from CLASS PRESIDENT by Johanna Hurwitz. Text copyright © 1990 by Johanna Hurwitz. By permission of Morrow Junior Books, a division of William Morrow & Company, Inc.

"The House on Hillside Lane" from ALDO APPLESAUCE by Johanna Hurwitz. Text copyright © 1979 by Johanna Hurwitz. By permission of Morrow Junior Books, a division of William Morrow & Company, Inc.

Text and three illustrations from MING LO MOVES THE MOUNTAIN by Arnold Lobel. Copyright © 1982 by Arnold Lobel. By permission of Greenwillow Books, a division of William Morrow & Company, Inc.

"Field" from COUNTRY PIE by Frank Asch. Copyright © 1979 by Frank Asch. Used by permission of Greenwillow Books, a division of William Morrow & Company, Inc.

"City: San Francisco" and "Trip: San Francisco" by Langston Hughes. Copyright 1958 by Langston Hughes. Copyright © renewed 1986 by George Houston Bass. Used by permission of Harold Ober Associates Incorporated.

MR. GRIGGS' WORK by Cynthia Rylant. Text copyright © 1989 by Cynthia Rylant. Illustration copyright © 1989 by Julie Downing. All rights reserved. Reprinted by permission of Orchard Books, New York.

BRINGING THE RAIN TO KAPITI PLAIN retold by Verna Aardema. Text copyright © 1981 by Verna Aardema. Used by permission of Dial Books for Young Readers, a division of Penguin Books USA Inc. Recorded by permission of Curtis Brown Ltd.

BEFORE YOU CAME THIS WAY by Byrd Baylor. Copyright © 1969 by Byrd Baylor. Used by permission of Penguin USA Inc.

WHERE THE RIVER BEGINS by Thomas Locker. Copyright © 1984 by Thomas Locker. Reprinted by permission of Penguin USA Inc.

"Fambly Time" from NIGHT ON NEIGHBORHOOD STREET by Eloise Greenfield. Text copyright © 1991 by Eloise Greenfield. Reprinted by permission of Dial Books for Young Readers, a division of Penguin Books, USA Inc. Recorded by permission of Marie Brown Associates.

"Children of Long Ago" from CHILDREN OF LONG AGO by Lessie Jones Little. Text copyright © 1988 by Weston Little. Reprinted by permission of Philomel Books. Recorded by permission of Marie Brown Associates.

IN COAL COUNTRY by Judith Hendershot. Copyright © 1987 by Judith Hendershot. Reprinted by permission of Random House Inc.

"Rise and Shine (Give Yourself a Chance)" by Professor Rap. Copyright © 1990 Professor Rap. Used by permission of Professor Rap.

"The City Blues" from FOLK BLUES by Jerry Silverman. Copyright © 1983 by Saw Mill Music, Inc. Used by permission of Saw Mill Music, Inc.

Excerpts from IF YOU LIVED AT THE TIME OF THE GREAT SAN FRANCISCO EARTHQUAKE by Ellen Levine. Copyright © 1987 by Ellen Levine. Reprinted by permission of Scholastic Inc.

Excerpts from IF YOU WERE THERE WHEN THEY SIGNED THE CONSTITUTION by Elizabeth Levy. Copyright © 1987 by Elizabeth Levy. Reprinted by permission of of Scholastic Inc.

Excerpts from MY BEST FRIEND MEE-YUNG KIM *Meeting a Korean-American Family* by Dianne MacMillan and Dorothy Freeman. Copyright © 1989 by Dianne MacMillan and Dorothy Freeman. Reprinted by permission of Simon & Schuster.

Taken from the book *50 Simple Things Kids Can Do to Save the Earth* by John Javna. Copyright © 1990 by John Javna. Reprinted by permission of Andrews & McMeel. All rights reserved.

MUSIC, MUSIC FOR EVERYONE by Vera B. Williams. Copyright © 1984 by Vera B. Williams. By permission of Greenwillow Books, a division of William Morrow & Company, Inc.

Excerpt from JOHN HENRY: An American Legend by Ezra Jack Keats. Text copyright © 1965 by Ezra Jack Keats. Abridgement by arrangement with Alfred A. Knopf, Inc. Recorded by arrangement with Alfred A. Knopf.

Excerpt from THE PATCHWORK QUILT by Valerie Flournoy. Text copyright © 1985 by Valerie Flournoy. Reprinted by permission of Dial Books for Young Readers, a division of Penguin Books USA Inc.

Excerpt from YAGUA DAYS by Cruz Martel. Text copyright © 1976 by Cruz Martel. Reprinted by permission of Penguin USA.